W9-ADA-156

HEINRICH MANN
and His Public

HEINRICH MANN

AND HIS PUBLIC

A Socioliterary Study
of the Relationship between
an Author and his Public

By LORENZ WINTER

Translated by John Gorman

UNIVERSITY of MIAMI PRESS
Coral Gables, Florida

Originally published in Germany in 1965 as
Heinrich Mann und sein Publikum.Eine
literatursoziologische Studie zum Verhältnis
von Autor und Öffentlichkeit
© 1965 by Westdeutscher Verlag - Köln und Opladen

Copyright © 1970 by University of Miami Press
Library of Congress Catalog Card No. 72-81616
ISBN 0-87024-123-0

Designed by Bernard Lipsky
Manufactured in the United States of America

Contents

Preface to the
American Edition

THIS STUDY had its basis in a dissertation, presented at the University of Munich in 1963, dealing with the work and influence of Heinrich Mann. At first I had considerable reservations about offering to a larger reading public a work intended primarily for fellow scholars. If I have done so, it was because my reading of the German novelist made it quite clear to me that the great literary myths that sustain his work are still current in the world today, although on a somewhat smaller scale than was once the case.

We often speak of artistic freedom. We seldom ask, however, on behalf of which reason the writer, who was once grateful for the few poetic freedoms allowed him, can claim the privilege to artistic freedom in his conduct. We speak of the existential problems of an author, but do not know whether, how, and since when it has been possible to combine the life of an artist with the doings of a poet. Following Oscar Wilde's saying that good feelings make bad poems, we use form as a counterweight to intention, but forget the former word has its primary significance in the language of sportsmen and diplomats. For the sportsman, form or shape signifies technical perfection. For the diplomat, it designates perfect courtesy. Can literature base its existence solely on these two notions? Such a possibility seems no more likely than that literature should survive solely to fulfill its assignment to express the inexpressable—something which would certainly provide born poets and writers with sparse nourishment indeed. We prefer, after much consideration and in all modesty, to discount literary fame and immortality as relics of old-fashioned romanticism, but we ourselves retain our most trivial papers for at least ten years. Whatever survives beyond this time belongs to eternity and justifies a new edition.

Apart from some minor corrections as to logical or terminological conclusiveness in the text of this book and the rejection of a few erroneous data in the bibliography, this edition corresponds fully to the original German edition.

Munich
Spring 1970

[Publisher's Note: This translation was thoroughly checked and in some instances revised by the author.]

HEINRICH MANN
and His Public

Introduction

THE introduction to this study of Heinrich Mann does not propose to offer anything more than a brief justification of its methods and goals. As is frequently the case with introductions, it was written after the book was finished. The reader may therefore hold it in abeyance until he has read the following chapters, and should seek, perhaps, answers to questions that arise beyond the horizon of the interpretation itself. The introduction, however, must stand at the beginning of the text, because socioliterary efforts are still in need of special justification. Literary scholars usually regard them with the suspicion that they touch only superficially on the essence of literature, while, on the other hand, many sociologists are vaguely distrustful of any preoccupation with the indeterminate products of literature.

This persistent opposition between the two disciplines seems rather remarkable since, in practice, their representatives are constantly working with one another's tools and methods. For the literary scholar it is a standard procedure to view "literature" as a complex social panorama composed of the printing and publishing trade, book selling and reviewing, academies, prize juries, literary conspiracies, public libraries, and similar factors. No scientist, on the other hand, however sober and dedicated in his devotion to the real world around him, has ever doubted that "sociology" may principally consist of paper and printer's ink—the classic products of men of letters. It is, therefore, basically unimportant which of these two worlds one views as real or fictitious. We may only be assured that these spheres will remain separate as long as scholars, in their experience, find it necessary to describe them with two quite different sets of concepts. The peculiar dialetical relationship between these two worlds remains, for the time being, truly amazing. It would be an enormous help to literary sociology if it could be recognized that essential statements about content, not only in the case of literature but elsewhere as well, either cannot be made at all or can be made only by using a language quite different from the language of this content. In the previous century one usually spoke "about" literature in the language of the historian. In this century we have added the language of the sociologist. It is incomprehensible that this language should be denied equal attention and recognition.

The concept "literature" is presently being replaced by that of "literary work of art." This expression is ambiguous. It has, on the one hand, a selective function in that it programmatically ascribes the rank of aesthetic perfection to a few of the vast multitude of literary works. A selective criterion of this sort, changing from case to case, obviously becomes necessary as soon as a highly developed technology brings about a vast increase in the number of printed works. The question, however, arises as to whether such works of a "literary" nature really exist, or even can exist, amidst the multitude of artistic products. The other rather common expression, "linguistic art work," betrays the same uncertainty. Lessing and Goethe were well aware that the plastic arts and music, because of their amorphous materials, could aim at the creation of definite products, while literature had to work with a pre-structured instrument, i.e., language, which is a tool to express personal moods, to depict material circumstances, to influence human environment, or to meditate about oneself, the world, and God. It is by no means self-evident that language—whether spoken or written—can ever give up its instrumental character to become a pure aesthetic product since, viewed as a material product, literature consists only of black lines on paper.

Of all the questions which sociology asks of literature, the most ticklish is probably that of the communicative value of literature in relation to society. In this usage, the concept of communication is supposed to embrace all four of the previously mentioned instrumental properties of the language that lie at the base of literature, without limitation as to whether the communication be intentional or not. The oft-repeated assertion that literature is not intended as communication is apparently a demand for the recognition of a special kind of literary communication that may be said to give no information and open no lines of communication. Yet this seemingly abstruse demand is not snatched out of the thin air of philological speculation but rather arises out of an actual historical "case": the aestheticism flourishing at the turn of the century. We may see here one of the many instances in which the critical theories of an era are obligingly constructed to meet the demands of the actual writing practices of an earlier time. The peculiar area of tension into which the concept of literature has moved as a result of this theory is a consequence of the fact that the special case mentioned above is possible only as a postulate, never as a verifiable fact. As soon as we make the qualification of literature as a purely aesthetic work dependent upon being communicative only of its own noncommunicative nature, we meet the resistance of language, which on occasion may not make any sense but will always have something to say. There have been some periods in German literature that were nourished only by the radiations from this tension. Yet there have

also been other times in which this tension seemed to have
died away completely. In addition, a public that categorically
rejects any attempt to define literature through its own relationship to a given readership provides, by its rigid attitude
toward literature, the best possible justification for assuming
the existence of such a relationship.

In this interpretation, the sociologist will see a case study;
the literary scholar, an intellectual biography. Both definitions express the purposes of this study very well. Despite the
fact that the discussion is limited to only part of Heinrich
Mann's works, the study is arranged chronologically. Yet
each of the chapters covers a separate problem. This method
is quite natural. The professional writer's view of his task at
twenty is very different from his outlook at forty or at sixty.
Likewise, in the course of his life, his work comes to fulfill
different functions for the public. The special interest of the
sociologist begins at the point when these functions are no
longer determined solely by biographical variables.

The first chapter is concerned primarily with the question
of how the original contact is made between a newly arising
author and his public. In his essay on literature, Sartre has
called this process *engagement,* or connection.[1] Since Sartre,
on account of certain philosophical considerations, gave a
one-sided emphasis to the engagement of the author only, it
was unavoidable that later critics would often misuse the
concept he had introduced into the discussion. Engagement
was often identified with political commitment—something
which is quite absurd since political commitment has, in itself, nothing whatever to do with the specific activity of the
writer as such. Sartre's essay, however, does show that its
author, although he himself admits that he never wanted to
make even "a superficial attempt at sociological explanation,"[2] always had in mind the problem of mutual engagement, or action and reaction between author and public.
These mutual influences seem to continue beyond the death

of an author and of his contemporary public. It is one of the most characteristic marks of our Western culture that it gives an independent value to the work of an author and tries hard to traditionalize this value, even though the work itself was originally only an awkward means of establishing contact between an author and the public. The "connection" between a deceased author and the public of later days is certainly related only indirectly to the events of socioliterary life described by Sartre. The first chapter is therefore primarily concerned with the contact between the author Heinrich Mann and the public of his time, although, as a reader, he was trying to cope with traditional values himself.

For just this reason, the first of the following chapters deals with the widest variety of material, as it has to cover not only the works the author completed between his twentieth and fortieth birthdays but also his literary background and preparation. It is obvious that both Nietzsche and Wagner play an important role here. We may also mention Heinrich Mann becoming engrossed with the writings of Ernest Renan and Wilhelm Dilthey as well as with Oswald Spengler during the twenties. Moreover, the early period of the author's life is far more important biographically and sociologically than the size of the chapter might indicate. During this time, Mann not only grew to human maturity and perfected his technical skill but found himself as an author as well. The forty-year-old writer of *Die kleine Stadt* had completed his development from reader to author, a development which everyone who feels a calling to write must complete and can afford to pass through only once and irrevocably. After the completion of this novel, he embodied the social fiction of a "writer," certified by his contemporaries. For this reason, the sudden end of the civil and civilian period in Germany shortly afterwards did not merely make him complain but also gave him cause for thanks as the historical break allowed him to see the old social fictions in sharp and plastic outline and to become more assured of his own life's achievement. Other writers, such as Paul Heyse and Emmanuel Geibel, whom Mann still respected, lacked this historical perception entirely and, in the final days of their existence as writers, seemed to be playing a social role that was outdated in the truest sense of the word.

Heinrich Mann became a "writer" during the heydey of the literary aestheticism at the turn of the century. This literary movement had originated in France and then been imported into Germany. Its only announced purpose was the proof of its own lack of purpose—a demonstrative posture that gave rise to the slogan that art was a purpose in itself. This slogan corresponded fully to the social role assigned to poets and writers as beings who were useless, yet somehow indispensable, for the world of solid citizens "gathered 'round the banners of production."[3] As the ladies of the era heard the compliments of sweet uselessness almost daily from their admirers and husbands, this may well explain the social composition of the reading public. The connection between an author and the public, however, also included the potential readership, even if these persons rarely picked up a book at all. The "feet-on-the-rail" type businessman was yet well acquainted with the only seasonable type of "poet." Thus the uncommunicative communication or the purposeless purpose was the virtue which the author of those days had to make out of the necessity of the unread author. The better he succeeded in this, the more his personal achievement came to the fore. This attitude of the author is called his distance as a writer from society. Such an attitude naturally required the existence of an individualistic ideology shared by his public. Though the writer had thus programmatically removed himself from society, he was thoroughly integrated into his public thanks to their common ideology. His potential readership expected him to take this attitude and no other. If this readership, despite its previous resolution not to waste time with anything so foolish as literature, actually picked up a book, it was by no means surprised to find there the profoundly meaningful silence of "art." Perhaps the realization that some person whom they had thought irreproachable in this respect was actually exerting himself to take on the despised role of "writer" would occasionally cause them to raise an eyebrow in suspicion. In any event, the example of Heinrich Mann shows that the situation of an unread author is by no means the same as that of one who is misunderstood or one who is despised. To be sure, the creative writer, in his own opinion, has "nothing to say." This estrangement between author and public did not, however, lead to the production of obvious nonsense on his part, nor did the public's low opinion of the writer bring him any reproach beyond that of being useless.

Perhaps a short general application of this idea might be useful at this point. The ability to read and write provides an unmistakable mark of social status not only in the bourgeois world, i.e., in a society oriented in principle toward material profit. But if we limit our regard to this society, we find that the man of letters had difficulty in demonstrating his usefulness there and hence had to resort to using the bourgeois pride in education as a weapon against the bourgeoisie. Consequently, he and his colleagues created a literature that was inaccessible to those persons having only the ability to read and write. The naive distinction between the educated man and the primitive, between the literate and the illiterate, was thereby converted to a gap between the aesthete and the philistine, a situation in which, as mentioned above, the keeping of distance as a subjective act is not identical with the objective state of estrangement. As a result of this act, writing was no longer merely one of many ways of expressing life but rather came to be the source of a special position for the creative writer among his fellow men.

The chief characteristics of the artist are his irresponsibility and his daring. The man on the tightrope can never justify his groundless folly to the audience, and only a few of them will, like him, challenge the rest of their fellowmen by a daring that takes no account of the deeply mankind's need for security. The tightrope walker is alone, answerable only to himself, and is the object of blind, unconditional admiration. This figure was the perfect ideal for the literary artist. To be sure, he imitated the tightrope walker only symbolically, and the novel offered him fewer opportunities for this symbolic imitation than did poetry. In Heinrich Mann, there was added a traditional distaste for the bohemian flightiness of the artist and a critical sense for affectations.

His novels, therefore, were never mere expressions but always examples and critical counterexamples of literary aestheticism. His dialogue technique of telling the story, which relieved the author of responsibility for what was said, contradicted the reflective style of what the speakers expressed. In any event, the relationship of the literary artist to his public was more complex than that of the tightrope walker. To be sure, his constant effort to be in good "form" or shape earned him a respect somewhat tinged with fear. But, as readers were accustomed to demand more than mere sport from a writer, the relationship between writer and public continued to be sustained by an unsatisfied tension, even where people were willing to accept the fact that the artist embodied the only possible form of existence for a contemporary writer. Since the inheritance of a morally colored tradition from the past was so much stronger than the most generous cultural liberalism, Goethe, whom Eichendorff reproached for having artistic tendencies, disagreed strongly, as both a writer and a critic, with any attempt to measure the cultural level of a people according to its understanding of ballet and circus.[4]

When the creative writer climbs onto the tightrope and, in this fashion, lets literature step forward as the proof of its own purposelessness, the language of his writings tends to change from a tool to a product. As a product, language directs attention to nothing but itself. But a product, in contrast to a tool, is destined to consumption. Artistic literature, therefore, was a slave to a type of consumption, which, although only symbolic, could go as far as wanton destruction. Consumption, however, was the proverbial red flag for the bourgeoisie, and it filled them with fear and terror. Only one other red flag could cause such unseemly excitement: the banner of the Socialist parties. To the burgher, both unrestrained consumption and socialism, in the hands of the writer, signified sheer terror. For the workers, who stood beside him in ever increasing numbers, they meant a rhetoric that promised much and imposed no obligations. Beside the artistic aestheticism of the day, the political aestheticism represented no unusual mental attitude. It merely provided the creative writer with a daily penance to lighten a conscience burdened by so many sinful excesses.

Heinrich Mann took up the theme of socialism very late in his career and never adopted it as his artistic credo. In *Im Schlaraffenland* (1901), this catchword was the butt of jokes. In *Die Jagd nach Liebe* (1903), persons who took it seriously were objects of pity. In *Zwischen den Rassen*, there was certainly much enthusiasm for a "new state," which might have been expected, as one of the figures in the previous work, *Die Göttinnen,* had already come over to the side of the Italian *Risorgimento.* The nature of this new state is shown in *Die kleine Stadt* (1909), which was the only one of Mann's books written in the style of political aestheticism. It proved to be rather old-fashioned, resembling the village idyll of the nineteenth century. Whatever comment Mann later made on historical events gained its significance from the name he had made for himself. His politics had virtually no effect on his conception of literature.

Chapters II and III take up the problems of fame and

immortality. As the title of this study suggests, the discussions therein are more of the nature of examples than of basic explanations. Yet the example of Heinrich Mann does appear to have special weight in these areas as well. When he is discussed today, three works are mentioned: the film *Der blaue Engel,* the book on which it is based, *Professor Unrat,* and perhaps the novel *Der Untertan,* which has also been filmed. These works created the common picture of Mann as the "satirist of Wilhelminian Germany," a notion which the UFA film by Josef von Sternberg (1930) directly contradicts. (The DEFA film version of *Der Untertan,* done twenty years later by Wolfgang Staudte, is far closer to the original work.) Here we are dealing with an *ex post facto* adoption of the author by the reading public, in which the old Roman proverb about books having their own fate applies perfectly. Often this later adoption can be seen in the incorporation of an author's works into the programs of popular book clubs, reading circles, etc. The popularity of such organizations rests by no means on their supposedly low level of taste, but rather, as Robert Escarpit[5] has shown, on the opportunity they offer to their members of refusing to see the original historical situation of the authors they serve up. The program of the book club puts all writers into the same social present. It makes them, as the saying goes, timeless.

Heinrich Mann knew that he could allow himself a novel like *Der Untertan* only at the peak of his career. He could certainly have had no idea of how the events of 1914 would affect the reputation of the book, which, although finished, had not yet been published in its entirety. The result was his ten year struggle with his own legend, to which we owe two additional novels and perhaps a half dozen essays.

The socioliterary stereotype that is formed when a writer is taken up by the public evades any evaluation. This phantom is no longer under the writer's control, although it lies in wait for him at every street corner and denies and mocks his most secret wishes. It is the hobgoblin of a "mission" that echoes and reechoes until the writer becomes his own legend, and his only remaining consolation is the knowledge that his earlier development to authorship constituted a "creative betrayal"[6] of the same magnitude. If, in the happy days of his youth, the public had rubbed its eyes in astonishment at the sight of a finished writer, that surprise was the result of the author's betrayal of the hopes that his contemporaries had held for him. When the storm of events of 1914 had blown over, Heinrich Mann reconciled himself to his legend and even helped it along as best he could in the hope of giving permanence to his work.

Around the middle of the last century, writers were accustomed to draw blank checks on the future. That future would overthrow the bourgeois world, which supposedly had neither the inclination nor the understanding for higher things. Before the tribunal of the future, these writers hoped to win their "appeal." Heinrich Mann experienced the end of the bourgeois world personally. He became aware of this end even in those writings which he later always regarded with a certain embarassment, i.e., his pessimistic cultural essays in the magazine *Das Zwanzigste Jahrhundert* and his first novel, *In einer Familie.* What made these youthful works painful to recall was the provincial perspective with which he had observed the events of the day. A novel like the supposedly prophetic *Der Untertan,* which praised the old bourgeois ideal, appears to us today far more "reactionary" than the immediate struggle with the march of time in the somewhat unpolished earlier work.

The end of the bourgeois world was not a cataclysm like the First World War, which only signaled this event around the world, but it was also more than the sum total of a series of palace revolutions plus a currency reform. It was the silent end of a representative western and central European way of life, an event which even the sociopolitical vocabulary handed down to us today cannot deny. Heinrich Mann lived as a burgher during his own lifetime and thus was able, for awhile at least, to observe from the underworld just how long a bourgeois literature would last. For him, as for the other survivors among the adherents of the old way of life, the future was full of unknown threats rather than encouraging promises. The ideas he had received in proud consciousness of their eternal validity or their visionary anticipation of the future could crumble even faster than the paper they were written on.

Heinrich Mann answered these threats with renewed struggles. First in the limited frame of the generation gap, then on the larger canvas of historical parable, the fifty-year-old author discovered his personal transientness, which he sought to avoid through cunning and trickery. This discovery gave rise to his later production, composed mostly of books about books, including his own. This technique showed neither frivolity nor stubborness. The author has a perfect right to point out to inattentive readers that books are really the result of struggles and that they are "fruitful imbalances,"[7] which nature and history can always set right again. Thus the question of literary duration should lead even the sociologist into the literary role of the conscientious reader.

In his essay on literature Sartre writes that every work produced by the intellect contains the image of the reader for whom it is intended.[8] Although this thesis is intended as a general statement, it naturally takes on a certain charm when it may be taken literally, e.g., in the study of novels that present a fictional public or in some way deal directly with the relationship between author and reader. From this point of view, the texts to be interpreted were selected. All of them contain the motif of the reception of art in completed form or at least in a series of pregnant episodes. In our opinion, this element leads the reader into the deepest meaning of literature—which does not consist in the uncommunicative communication or the purposeless purpose but rather in the fact that everything described in literature is in fact an invention of the author, or that the author, as Sartre puts it, is actually creating something, although the reader may think he is merely watching him reveal already given factual data. This idea corresponds exactly to the sociological conception of the role of the creative writer in our society. The public expects him to invent something new and, indeed, allows him a categorical freedom of decision in his art. Yet it still feels authorized to call him to account for his deeds from time to time in rather rough fashion.

By way of conclusion I would like to say something about the collective concept of "bourgeois literature," which obviously embraces printed works of the most varied historical, social, and aesthetic styles. This phrase refers not so much to that which is written by or about the bourgeoisie but rather to what is written for the bourgeoisie. To speak more exactly, it designates everything written for the bourgeois public or, practically speaking, the literature produced from the end of the Thirty Years' War up to the outbreak of World War I. These two centuries and a half have indeed produced a variety of writing styles but, remarkably enough, only one style of reading, which prevails even today. This style of reading, however, has long since lost all those social conditions that kept it alive: the printed word as the only widespread means of communication, literature as the embodiment of the nationally recognized official language, and a great reservoir of illiterates whose steadily rising level of education since the Middle Ages had greatly stimulated the demand for literature. It was this very realization that the reservoir of the illiterate was shrinking that caused bourgeois men of letters to resort to an erudition and mastery of form that was inaccessible to the so-called average reader. During the Middle Ages, when the mere ability to read and write made one "educated," such a reaction would have been unnecessary. In the Western world of today, where this ability is virtually universal, it is impossible. The position of literature in this world, therefore, can no longer be determined by the old dispute of the writers as to whether writing is a public concern or an inalienable self expression of the author. This question would presuppose the critic's adherence to the old style of reading, which was significant for the recently educated—but never fully canonized—reader.

1 From Reader to Author (1894-1909)

Das Zwanzigste Jahrhundert,
In einer Familie,
Im Schlaraffenland,
Die kleine Stadt

TOWARD the end of his life, Heinrich Mann wrote: "If I had firm convictions, and basically I held the same ones from early youth onward, I believed myself obliged to form them." A few lines below he added: "One receives a religion very early in life, learns to judge it properly, and yet retains it, or at least its memory, until the end."[1] In view of these confessions—which draw the self-portrait of an author who, despite all his formal perfections, always tried to remain true to his inherited view of life and the world—it seems necessary to examine quite closely the social and literary circumstances accompanying his first appearance as an author.

Heinrich Mann's youth was also the youth of a literary generation that felt an unusual sense of community based on origin, status, and profession. Before the arrival of this new wave of writers roughly around 1900, the "high class" literature of Germany had felt no fresh impulses for twenty years. The extraordinary generational gap between Wilhelm Raabe (born in 1831) and Gerhart Hauptmann (born in 1862), which has no parallel in the history of more recent German literature, must have been felt in the second half of the nineteenth century in the form of a noticeable aging of "high class" literature.[2] Obviously, the revolution of 1848, which fell between those dates, had led not only to a new sociopolitical orientation but to new directions in literature as well, which denied to all those young would-be authors a spontaneous attachment to an inherited tradition. Also the bourgeoisie, busy with more important things than literature, could not immediately assume the role that princely patrons had played for Klopstock, Heinse, Goethe, Schiller, Jean Paul, Kleist, Tieck, Wagner, Heyse, Geibel, et al. The laborious "collective patronage" provided by well-known individual publishers of the eighteenth and nineteenth centuries, like Cotta or Campe, which today seems wholly incommensurate with the potentialities of the publishing trade, and which certainly did not replace the "noncommercial" support of noble and princely patrons, shows clearly how much time was required for the development of bourgeois literature into a functioning social system. The literary generation that came to manhood around the turn of the century was, on the other hand, once again happy in the knowledge that its livelihood was assured and that it need not fear the fate of those nineteenth-century authors to whom the gracious patronage of the nobility had been denied. Although these writers were thoroughly bourgeois in origin and were sustained by money from their families, or by a bourgeois profession, or by a position with one of the flourishing literary magazines of the time, they nonetheless found time for frivolous occupations.[3] To be sure, they had to defend their poetic callings against the prosaic verdict of the bourgeois society. But, as the middle-class citizenry gradually came to acquire a taste for supporting its illustrious sons, a moderate success might ultimately justify the writer's choice of his occupation.

In the world of the rising literary generation, the large cities set the tone in all matters of convention, even for literature. Since the revolution of 1848 and the founding of the empire in 1871, the large cities had become the center of interest as economic, political, social, and literary focal points. Between these centers, there arose new forms of social connections that weakened the traditional orientation of the hinterland toward the local seat of government. As a result of this development, the generation gap was followed by the simultaneous growth of both a "high class" and a "lower class" literature. The "lower class" literature was represented not by the authors of vulgar trivia but rather by the more conservative writers of the rustic homeland on the one hand, and, on the other, by the more progressive urban literary artisans. In the realm of "high class" literature, this opposition of genres had already made itself known during the first half of the nineteenth century, especially in the simultaneous activities of Heine and of the adherents of poetic realism. Among the homeland writers, the generation gap was more clearly visible, a sign that this form needed a longer time to determine its position and to adjust to it. Peter Rosegger (born in 1843) still was almost the equal of Stifter in public esteem while Heinrich Sohnrey and J. C. Heer had already sunk far below this. The first generation of naturalists, partly bohemian and partly proletarian in character, e.g., the Hart brothers, Bleibtreu, Kretzer, Wolzogen, or Sudermann (all born between 1854 and 1859), could take advantage of the opportunities offered by the gradually urbanizing culture around them. But, in common with the somewhat younger naturalists proper (Holz, Schlaf, Hartleben, Conradi, Halbe, et al.), most of them just as quickly became victims of the overabundance of literary talent that had been attracted to the cities. Of the Hauptmann brothers, only the younger, after years of struggle, succeeded in holding himself on the surface of literary life. Around the turn of the century, opportunities for distinguishing oneself as an individual had become so rare that Hugo von Hofmannsthal could describe the magazine *Neue Rundschau* as an overcrowded swimming pool. If, after the dryness and lack in color of previous decades, the new age could be greeted with flash and splendor, and prolific treasure of invention, it was a result of the fact that the inhabitants of the literary world were compelled to work under enormous competitive pressure. Consequently, satires, quarrels, and feuds were the order of the day. Very common, however, was the rapid formation of groups, which began with the literary societies of naturalism (Durch, Freie literarische Gesellschaft, Gesellschaft für modernes Leben) and went on to the circle around Stefan George, as it was only through uniting their powers that writers with similar inclinations and talents could preserve themselves from mutual ruin.

Both the literary and the political worlds of late nineteenth-century Germany were thus in a state of flux. Older authors had often grown into local monuments, thanks to their connections with the smaller princely courts or with the free cities of the empire, and could therefore feel assured of enriching either the classical "Weltliterature" or the romantic "Universalpoesie" after their deaths. From the perspective of the 1890s, however, all previous "eternal values" seemed to be fading rapidly away.

We can well imagine what impression this world made on Heinrich Mann, the well-bred son of a solid citizen of Lübeck, who had decided to become a writer. Like most other members of his generation, he had to draw his historical model from the first half of the nineteenth century, and consequently he shared the general idea of that time as to "how long a gifted author must reasonably expect to remain unknown [and] at what age he is normally crowned with fame." [4] Thus he saw the contemporary events as a clear threat to his own future.

"Naturalism, mysticism, social literature, romantic fantasies, cynical realism, and escapist yearning for beauty and faith—so many paths run through the land of modern literature that one finally loses his way. . . . Where is the right way that leads into the future of literature?" Heinrich Mann wondered in 1896 in the name of many of his contemporaries.[5] The literary generation of the turn of the century would have been quite incapable of determining its canon of "high class" literature for quite some time to come had it not possessed a single common teacher: Friedrich Nietzsche, who was, at that time, probably the only widely discussed author of rank in Germany. Nietzsche, who was, by profession, a professor of ancient philology and not a writer, owed his more or less great influence on writers as varied as the Mann brothers, Frank Wedekind, Stefan George, Hugo von Hofmannsthal, Rainer Maria Rilke, Hermann Hesse, et al., less to his aesthetic achievements than to his peculiar historical position. Nietzsche was born in 1844 in the midst of the generational gap and, perhaps for this reason, never really became a creative writer, but chiefly took on the task of an intermediary and guardian, thus acting as a *poeta doctus* of excellence. His painstakingly developed idea of the aristocracy illuminated a world which he had seen smashed in his childhood but which he still felt it his mission to live in. If the literary generation of the turn of the century took from Nietzsche's doctrines this very idea of aristocracy and raised it to the rank of chief hallmark of their literary canon, they were by no means continuing with any given literary tradition.

The connection between bourgeois literature and aristocracy in the first half of the nineteenth century came about through the fact that it was only by way of literature that the burgher could reach the world of the nobility and, as a writer or an artist, so escape his inherited social stigma. For the older authors, in view of their financial dependence, it would have been ridiculous, if not even dangerous, to exceed the boundaries set by their patrons. Aristocracy was not their personal way of life but rather a moral code conceded without envy to their masters. Heinrich Mann once called attention to Goethe's confession that, for his entire life, he had felt embarassed in the presence even of an officer of minor nobility.[6] Nietzsche's outlook differed from this attitude since, in his own time, the quasi-feudal personal bonds between patrons and artists had been almost completely torn, and he could only dedicate his heroic and mythical remembrances to the "great" days of the past.

It was by way of his constant dedication that the idea of aristocracy found its way into literature, no other models being available. But this idea was not merely an expression of the newly-awakened social consciousness of the burghers' sons, who, far from being ashamed of their origins, were filled with the assurances of the superiority of bourgeois culture. Moreover, the creative writer now found an aristocratic bearing a necessary compensation for his choice of a profession despised by his fellow citizens. The aristocratic mannerisms of an author of the early nineteenth century were a *social* convention, independent of the specific activity of the author as such. In the sense of this convention, writing served as a means of making the burgher appear worthy of nobility on account of his literary activity. The aristocratic bearing and mannerisms of the authors of the late nineteenth century, on the other hand, existed as a literary convention of quite uncertain validity and endurance; the task of making the unworthy trade of writing look respectable to the burghers could not be isolated from the literary act proper. By means of his canon of "high class" literature, the "artist" adopted with regard to the "burgher" those privileges that the true nobility had once possessed. Furthermore, since one of these privileges stated that only the aristocracy might spend money on art, the artist at the turn of the century knew no more pressing duty than that of convincing the bourgeoisie that this privilege had come down to him as the sole remaining *arbiter elegantiarum.*[7]

Still another model appeared on the sociointellectual

horizon to the searching look of the younger generation. Nietzsche had been moved to literary activity in the narrower sense, and thereby away from his own profession, by his encounter with Richard Wagner, for whose idea of *Gesamtkunstwerk* he supplied the theoretical outline in his *Geburt der Tragödie aus dem Geiste der Musik* (1872). Thus, the composer of operas took his place beside the scholar of ancient philology in helping to fill the vacuum of "high class" literature in the seventies and eighties. While Nietzsche succeeded in providing the younger generation with its literary canon and with the fiction of an unbroken tradition of "high class" literature, Wagner's art form served to bring that canon indirectly to the attention of sections of the public which ordinarily cared little for the subtleties of literary technique. At Bayreuth, the aesthetic aristocracy obtained that minimum of public representation that was necessary to make it a sanctified institution, despite all its "wickedness." Wagner's person and work gave his contemporaries no fewer puzzles than the philosophical literary efforts of the man who was first his friend and later his intimate enemy. Although he was thirty years older than Nietzsche and musically still tied in part to the romantic period, Wagner, as an author, took the side of a revolution that could break out at any time, while Nietzsche strove in vain to drive it out of his consciousness. In his theoretical writings, *Die Kunst und die Revolution* and *Das Kunstwerk der Zukunft* (1849-1850), Wagner gave the clearest proof that he knew how to interpret the signs of the times. The political tactic of the economically independent bourgeoisie of allying themselves with the people, i.e., with its less wealthy contemporaries whose help was necessary for its rise, found its expression with Wagner in his idea of a national drama and a folk theater as of classical antiquity.

In any event, Wagner, always a practical thinker, did not hesitate, after the "revolution" was complete, in breaking off his flirtation with the folk and in dedicating his artistic creations exclusively to the newly arisen bourgeois public. An exasperated editor of a conservative provincial magazine stated firmly: "Thus, we Germans, instead of a national theater, have received a fashionable international health resort for worn out epicures, emancipated American women, zany Englishmen, and old biddies."[8]

But Wagner was filling not only a psychic but also a social need of his audience. The fact that the work of an opera composer should sound forth into the increasing stillness of "high class" literature between 1870 and 1890 fitted in very well with the increasing centralization of culture in the cities, which had begun with the rise of the bourgeoisie after 1850. Likewise and in harmony with this general development, the "Freie Bühne," the theatrical podium of the naturalist movement in Berlin, although based on a quite different intellectual concept, cherished the same social exclusiveness as the neobaroque festivities of Bayreuth or the court-oriented Prussian art of Wildenbruch. In a certain way, the movement toward social exclusiveness in the realm of the theater and the inclination toward aesthetic aristocracy in literature were parallel appearances. While Wagner's art reached a select group of hearers, the works of Nietzsche reassembled the cast of literary actors. Totally independent of this activity, Nietzsche, as Thomas Mann noted, was able to operate in respect to politics as the spokesman for the middle class."[9]

Through his two years as publisher of the magazine *Das Zwanzigste Jahrhundert,* the twenty-four-year old Heinrich Mann happened to get, at the very start of his literary career, into the circle of the "Alldeutscher Verband" (founded in 1891), whose sociopolitical program consisted of an alliance of the nobility with the "aristocratic non-nobles" against the liberal capitalistic bourgeoisie. [10] Since most of Mann's contributions to the magazine appeared in the form of book and play reviews and therefore show him more in the role of a reader and critic than in that of a creative writer, a comparative look at his first novel, *In einer Familie,* published in 1894, must be taken to get an idea of his personal concept of the position of the writer in society.

The majority of the later adherents of the canon of "high class" literature found, as they entered the literary world, that it was split into the two camps of urban literature and literature of the rustic homeland. They recognized that the path of naturalism was too well-worn and the path of regionalism too remote to reach the attention of the educated public. Sailing carefully between the Scylla of banality and the Charibdis of mere scurrility, they discovered their task in impressing the urban public with their provincial and therefore almost feudal origins, while at the same time not neglecting to meet the educated provincial with cosmopolitan indolence and the better manners of the metropolis. Without a doubt, Heinrich Mann personally acquired not only these characteristics but also a practical savoir faire arising out of his "knowledge of the market " gained during his year of apprenticeship in the book selling trade. He therefore praised in his magazine the "parochialism" of the ancients, of the Renaissance, and of Weimar classicism, which he felt had led to the "most unsurpassable states of culture,"[11] and, in the same fashion, chose Dresden over Berlin as the setting for his novel. Yet, despite the official direction of the magazine, he used its pages openly and comfortably to disseminate his knowledge of the "more hidden tendencies of the times" and took as the hero of his novel a man of inherited wealth, an aristocratic aesthete, one who was a "reactionary" in the Nietzschean sense.[12]

This man, Wellkamp, "scarcely regarded even truth and error as opposites and was content to accept everything." He read French authors, attended Wagner's *Tannhäuser,* and allowed himself to be led into adultery with an international socialite from the upper bourgeoisie; at the end of the novel, however, he was willing to accept the moral preachments of an upright, correct, and decent major and returned contritely to his good, lower middle-class wife. To his mistress he was drawn by "something more unresistable than any sort of physical attraction . . . the worship of a secret beauty . . . something which is forbidden in everyday life." Yet, when he received from her the work of a "wicked" author, the presentation offered a welcome opportunity to warn him to enjoy the book with care since its author had "already caused enough mischief among our youth of today by his total indifference and his intellectual tightrope walking."[13] In one of his magazine articles, Mann himself once treated this ambiguous attitude ironically when he distinguished between the "skeptics," for whom "a fine sense for form becomes all," and the "prophets," who consider it "a sin against the Holy Ghost not to share their healing truth with the whole world."[14]

In fact, Heinrich Mann's first novel, *In einer Familie,* and his articles in *Das Zwanzigste Jahrhundert* were, quite characteristically, a mixture of the prophetic and the skeptical, of both moral and aesthetic literature. The two types of literature would henceforth allow the author—though still with inadequate means[15] —to address himself in appropriate ways to different segments of the public and to recommend himself to them as an elevated writer who did not place his trust in worn-out clichés. From the editorial office of his conservative middle-class magazine and from the provincial peace of his novel, Heinrich Mann looked out with fascination on the wild ferment of the metropolis where the literature of the future was being made. Here lay both an opportunity and a danger. The modern city public, which knew its Maupassant and its Wagner, might perhaps have nodded encouragingly to a well meant aestheticism but would hardly have been outraged by it. It could therefore do no harm to reaffirm loudly from time to time not only that its liberal materialism was outdated, but also that the denial of God and immortality in favor of science and enlightenment was a "reactionary crime." Only among the readership of small town professionals Heinrich Mann could probably have aroused attention with the assertion that, property and education being provided, materialism was thoroughly acceptable as "the final explanation of the essence and purpose of things." [16] Yet this declaration of solidarity with his needy contemporaries was not allowed to infringe upon the freedom of "art" in any way. To be sure, the writer, like Nietzsche, could take sides with the bourgeoisie without reservation, but could not appear before it unconditionally. In this regard, it was proper to maintain a distance and to explain that respect was the principle of German idealism, the essence of German culture being "aristocratic, unchanging, and inexorably aristocratic." [17] In case of necessity this literary exclusiveness could always be defended by a censorship, which, although it left science and philosophy untouched, was still able to prevent "any knowledge of a temporary trespass of a scientific direction on the untouchable domain of faith from finding its way to the lower levels of the populace." [18]

In an autobiographical letter written in 1943, Heinrich Mann admitted: "At twenty, I could do nothing at all. Around thirty, with *Im Schlaraffenland,* I learned ... the technique of the novel." [19] Programmatically, this "novel among fine people," published punctually at the turn of the century, still showed a certain affinity to his previous writings. But, looked at from a purely professional point of view, the novel carried its author over more than a hundred years from his former stylized emulation of Goethe into his personal experience of the modern era. This leap may be explained as the result of Mann's development from reader to author that had taken place in the meantime. In his magazine articles as well as in his first novel, he had depicted himself as a well-versed reader by quoting well-known artists and making references to contemporary ideas and events. But, by retaining his conservative viewpoint, he had let it be known that his flexibility had never sunk to the level of mere routine. *Im Schlaraffenland,* for the first time, imposed this ambiguous attitude completely upon its readers by forcing them to accept a conservative verdict on certain questions of the day in a literary language whose modernity stood in glaring contrast to that verdict.

Im Schlaraffenland was mainly the story of the "resistable rise" of young Andreas Zumsee, heir to a Rhineish vineyard and candidate for a teaching position, to the post of court poet of the world of stock exchange, press, and theater in the Berlin of 1893. Heinrich Mann had announced the story of this promising talent some years before the appearance of the novel when he discussed the Alsatian poems of his colleague, Friedrich Lienhard, in *Das Zwanzigste Jahrhundert.* He used this opportunity to bewail at length the disillusionment felt by the hopeful arrival from the province at the sight of the coldness, triviality, false friendliness, and baseness that marked life in the large cities, and demanded that, for once, "a provincial healthiness" should "break over the capital like a spring thunderstorm."[20] Young Zumsee had thus to pride himself on his rustic feudal homeland and even on a sham Catholicism. But his creator also found it advisable to have the simple German small-town soul be a bit infected by worldly decadence. Zumsee, the successful "poet" who set up the remarkable aesthetics of "To feel, that is everything! What is the significance of perpetrating poems or of writing a novel? " and invoked Heine, Poe, Baudelaire, Verlaine, and Nietzsche as his authorities; the poet whose most vital concern was with outward appearances—men's fashions, massages, the fencing club, his visiting card, and his coat of arms; the aesthete, who enjoyed, with an "organ sensitive to the scarcely audible breath of the *Zeitgeist*. . . the yet unborn titillation of a high spiritual corruption," and who wandered along, "certainly not yet an aristocrat, but scarcely still part of the bourgeoisie"; the "artist," who, even after the surrender of his beloved, demanded yet more personal presents from her; and the "man of letters," who, despite the split in his own psyche, could take a questionable pleasure in pitying a stock broker for his bourgeois pangs of conscience and moral scruples. [21] All of these dandyisms followed exactly the aristocratic canon of aesthetic extravagance that Nietzsche had passed on to the bourgeois literature of *fin de siècle*. The wit of this literature consisted solely in the fact that the big city public of *Im Schlaraffenland* laughingly pardoned Zumsee's antics because they were part of his "artistic freedom."

Heinrich Mann's own ambition, however, reached farther than that of his "innocent upstart." He dreaded whether his follies, while amusing the metropolitan public, would win his author any respect in these quarters. More probably, the appearance of the young man of the world would have aroused far more admiration in the provinces than in Berlin, where it was feasible to indicate that his creator found his "villainies" basically cheap and repulsive. Therefore, Mann kept himself at a distance from Zumsee's behavior by means of an apparently parodistic treatment of this figure and the introduction of a conservative, moralistic counterpart in the form of the writer Friedrich Köpf, the truly "noble" character of the book. [22]

Köpf could shine through as the secret hero of the novel by being permanently and hence favorably absent. *Im Schlaraffenland* spoke the language of Zumsee, whom it backhandedly condemned though, while Köpf always stood in the wings, yet was permitted to make fun even of "the most sacred goods of the nation," such as the stock exchange. Politically, Zumsee believed in laissez faire, while Köpf's "bourgeois absolutism" was not so very far from the opinions of that magazine editor who had once called the denial of

God and immortality and the propagation of materialism and
atheism "a reactionary crime of the stock jobbers' press."
Thus it was probably not Zumsee's aesthetic deviations, but
rather the political moralism of Köpf, a residue of Mann's
own views as set forth in *Das Zwanzigste Jahrhundert*
(though carefully camouflaged beneath a veil of satire), that
helped make *Im Schlaraffenland* a "tiny sensation" in the
liberal Berlin of the turn of the century. The first review
reassured the readers, however, that no "twilight of the idols
of capitalism"[23] was taking place in the novel. At the same
time, the middle class, whose demise Heinrich Mann most
dutifully bewailed,[24] can be supposed to have been impressed
far more by the book's artistic extravagances than by its par-
tisanship on their behalf.

The technique of apparent parody, practiced not only on
Zumsee but also on almost all of the characters of the book
and distinguishing all of Mann's artistic novels, was thoroughly explained by the author in his essay on Flaubert as
the method to put his real opinions always in the mouth of a
person "whom I have so arranged that no one will believe
him."[25] By means of this remarkable technique, contact
with the public was indeed established, but this contact did
not result in a mutual attachment of author and reader, but
rather in a mutual detachment of one from the other—a detachment that first made possible their mutual perception. Above
all, the literary contact must never endanger the exclusiveness
of the writer. In this regard, Heinrich Mann, in his essay on
Flaubert, spoke of the "supposed absence" of the author in
his work, which had as its equivalent the notorious "inward
affection" of the bourgeois reader. Both partners in this communication were, therefore, to be found essentially beyond
their literary activities, which served more or less as a pretext.
The reader could therefore never fully comprehend the
author.

This peculiar process represents a double paradox. First of

all, there is the fact that the author demanded that his readers take him seriously, although he, for his part, did not take them seriously. On the contrary, he established himself as an *individuum* with all the privileges involved, first by his knowledge of the inferiority of those to whom he addressed his communication and who could do nothing in revenge but to laugh at the useless scratchings of the writer's pen. Secondly, the use of literature as a means of communication for the purpose of aesthetic detachment led to the paradox of publicly declared solitude and also to the conventionalization of the individualistic ideology insofar as such an ideology could only exist collectively, i.e., in a group of believers in that ideology. In the final analysis, the integration of even the most esoteric artist into society resulted simply from the general recognition of his program by that group.

As *Im Schlaraffenland* once again played off the aesthete against the moralist, Heinrich Mann still retained, just as in his first writings, the aloofness of the man of letters, not only from the liberal public of the cities but also from the conservative public of the provinces. Yet he was not indulging in mere literary frivolity when speaking for the artistic community, he "urgently demanded recognition from those whom [one] never acknowledged as jurors." [26] The aloofness of the man of letters from his public, like the special technique by which it arose, was certainly not Heinrich Mann's special discovery as an author but rather an idea he had picked up as a reader from other authors. When Köpf of *Im Schlaraffenland* felt obliged to defend the status of "true" literature against the importance given in Berlin to social connections, the press, and the theater, [27] he was voicing the judgment as to value, which the well-educated provincial usually makes in favor of the printed book even today. With a clear conscience Heinrich Mann could quite comfortably see in this reverence a manifestation of the principle of German idealism as an essentially aristocratic culture, not only because he wished to see this attitude in his own public, but also because he always returned to it himself, as soon as he took on the role of the reader and looked up to the "great masters" of the literary past.

It was therefore definitely of symbolic significance that the writings of the Church Fathers lay on Köpf's desk. The public of "true" literature was thereby defined as a flock of believers, while the writers took on the function of a secular priesthood. Heinrich Heine had already observed that many bourgeois writers of the eighteenth century had grown into the "role of the Church Fathers" in the wake of the French Revolution, a development that found its reverse equivalent in Germany in the fact that many bourgeois writers were the sons of Lutheran pastors. Literature, true to the medieval tradition, remained thus the property of a secularized clergy. The significance of this situation for the individual author becomes clear, however, only when we consider that his role, unlike that of the village pastor, was not sanctioned as an institution, so that he could never escape the feeling of being a heretic. From the perspective of the province in which Heinrich Mann had learned to study literature as a reader, the task of this new clergy, according to the traditional outlook, still consisted above all in providing a point of reference for a geographically scattered bourgeoisie, thus assisting in its political rise.

This task fitted in very well with the personal attachment of the author to the world of the nobility. For he was concerned not with a choice between two given parties but with the discoverey of a new public whose position in the politics of the eighteenth and early nineteenth centuries was by no means firm. Rousseau's distress over the misery of the French peasants and Goethe's vain protest against the hunting practices of the Weimar gentry were political manifestos within the frame of an order that they did not question in principle. [28] Their political activity went on quite independently of the bourgeoisie's literary coming to consciousness as a social group, toward which their books contributed. After this group had come into public view with the revolution, literature once again lost its special social function. If a young writer around 1900 compared his opportunities with those that had been available to prerevolutionary authors, he soon realized, as did Heinrich Mann, that there remained for him only the role of the skeptical aesthete or that of the moralizing political prophet. The first type, as a disciple of Nietzsche, would seek to preserve the aloofness of the literary clergy by converting the social aristocracy of the older authors into the literary canon of aesthetic consumption.[29] The second would heedlessly equate the social function of literature with the actual political questions available for discussion, and either take the part of those "disinherited" by the revolution or accept the "disinheriting" with resignation and remind the ruling circles of society of their political responsibilities.

This takes the reader directly to the heart of the ingenious staging of the naturalistic horror drama, *Rache!*, in *Im Schlaraffenland,* which contemporary Heinrich Mann research more or less unanimously takes to be a satire on the premier—not the play itself—of Gerhart Hauptmann's drama *Die Weber* at the Freie Bühne in Berlin. In a review of the play published some years earlier, Heinrich Mann had already reproached Hauptmann for being "hypnotized by the basic mood of socialist democracy." Yet the political consequences of the "play which is Social Democratic to the core"[30] seemed to be of far less concern to Mann than the possibility that such a play could put bourgeois culture at the mercy of barbarism if it fell into the wrong hands.[31] The horrifying picture of the decline of culture disseminated here is also found in almost literal correspondence in Nietzsche's *Geburt der Tragödie aus dem Geiste der Musik.*[32] This apprehension revealed a conflict of conscience that allowed Mann, the

middle-class reader, to respect the craft of writing only because of its onetime revolutionary social function, but which
made Mann, the aspiring author, conscious of his literary
exclusiveness, fear for the "canonical" structure and the
"eternal value" of literature. These disturbing feelings had
already appeared in Heine's work in his naive fear of the
repetition of the burning of the library at Alexandria by the
barbarians. [33] Actually, Heine knew that it was not a question of the material destruction of literature but rather one
of the historical replacement of one literary genre by
another. As a countermeasure, he suggested a basic "folk
education" for the public, forgetting, however, that this education, as soon as it was taken seriously by the individual,
would always be leading new disciples into the same conflict
of conscience.

The absurd applauding by millionaires of a *drama of
misery,* painstakingly caricatured by Heinrich Mann in his *Im
Schlaraffenland,* did not, however, conjure up such a sudden
decline of literature. The poverty of the weavers was "a
source of shame for enlightened citizens and for good Christians." [34] In applauding the depictor of this misery, Hauptmann, the bourgeois public was in accord with its refor-
matory duties. Yet, in 1890, the workers were far more
effectively represented through their party and welfare organizations than through the work of a bourgeois dramatist, so
that the one who profited most from the play was its author,
insofar as he was being permitted to express his opinion on
sociopolitical questions of the day with a freedom and clarity
undreamed of by the bourgeois writer of the past. It was the
burgher in Heinrich Mann who fought against this fact, while
the artist in him demanded that freedom with ever increasing
urgency.

The analysis of the technique with which Heinrich Mann
defended the aloofness of the man of letters was based upon
the idea of literature that he acquired in his youth, i.e., the

idea of "high class" literature, which he, as a member of the bourgeois public, had received from older authors. *Im Schlaraffenland* also proved that he knew how to judge each of his own works equally well as author and as reader. This reflective mannerism, by which an author is able to "estrange" himself from his own product, can often contribute essentially to the aesthetic perfection of his work. But it also chains an author to the past more tightly than any superficial adoption of definite material, motives, or forms from older literature since it puts him in the position of viewing the social function of the writer's craft from one single and irrevocable perspective.

Heinrich Mann appeared in the role of public and reader primarily in Köpf's attack upon the theater in favor of "real" literature. There is a biographical explanation to this plea: Mann's puritanical upbringing in which his meeting with the theatrical crowd had not been "planned for." [35] Such an educational principle is not to be wondered at. The printed book, which arose from the provincial bourgeoisie, had always been more highly valued by this class as a means of information about and connection with the world than the theater—which also, incidentally, made far greater financial demands than small towns could possibly satisfy. The theater is the artistic center of a society that wants to show itself off, that sees the highest aesthetic values in outward representation and ceremony, and is prepared to pay for them. For this reason, and on account of the financial outlays required, the theater belonged to the court and to the big cities and not among the thrifty, sober, and socially awkward inhabitants of small towns. Nonetheless, it would be a mistake to seek the motive for the many barbs of *Im Schlaraffenland*—launched not only against the naturalistic theater in particular but also against the dramatic form of language and presentation in general—in the personal desire for revenge harbored by a beginning author who was not yet accepted into the theater. In the course of his brief association with the S. Fischer publishing house, which was closely connected to the naturalistic Freie Bühne, before the start of his career as a writer, Heinrich Mann had surely become fairly well acquainted with the theater business, as he later admitted in an interview.[36] Yet this contact did not stimulate him to undertake any theatrical works of his own. On the contrary, he turned decidedly to narrative writing once he had determined to become a professional writer. The emphatically antique, almost Goethean style of *In einer Familie* was, therefore, also an announcement of his opinion that poetic ideals could not be realized in the contemporary theater.

When Heinrich Mann wanted to gain greater esteem for what he considered "true" literature, this term naturally meant for him primarily the novel, as the flourishing erudite prose of the middle class had always been held in high regard ever since the times of scholarly journalism in the Enlightenment. The novel, as the chief product of certain literary factories that had arisen in the train of great capital investments and the transition to industrial techniques and procedures in publishing, did not enjoy this respect. It was held even less in respect as it served "only" to entertain—a reproach that was not leveled at contemporary dramatic productions, although these were often hardly more profound, because they had at their disposal the impressive paraphernalia of the theater. Considering the respect for erudite prose prevalent in the bourgeois province, on one side, and the fascination with theatrical pomp prevalent in metropolitan society, on the other, the novel did not yet find easy acceptance with the public, even when it had long since become that art form manifested in the work of Heinrich Mann. Quite significantly, his early work was criticized, less for not being "German" enough (that was the chief argument of later political propaganda) than for being too close to the "tabloid novel." This type of work, no matter how great its artistic perfection, supposedly could not engage either author or reader "seriously" enough. Such a reproach weighed very heavily in Germany, and it was perhaps the fear of this criticism that led a popular writer like Karl May, who understood the psychology of his readers so well, to call his books "Tales of Travel," rather than "Novels of Travel."

The weight of Köpf's plea on behalf of "true" literature can be accurately measured only with the aid of the contradictory fact that the scene and dialogue construction and style of *Im Schlaraffenland*, as of many of Mann's later books, went far beyond the stage performance depicted in the novel. The resulting paradox of this situation was that Heinrich Mann, while caricaturing the dramatic art form and stage practice of the day, inclined more and more to dramatic style in his literary language. This paradox is fairly easily explained when regarded as a struggle between Heinrich Mann as reader and Heinrich Mann as writer. His distaste as a bourgeois reader for the theatrical was, for practical purposes, a repetition of the sentiments expressed in Rousseau's "Lettre sur les spectacles" about Molière's comedies. This opinion favored a bourgeois "inner" experience of art, as opposed to a courtly "external" rite of form. [37] Mann's attitude as reader demanded the active participation of the reader in his reading and, in addition, his participation in a system of social "rules of the game" that, to be sure, had actually been revolutionary in effect during the eighteenth and early nineteenth centuries.

But, as an artistic author, Heinrich Mann gradually began to free himself from these traditional views of literature. Without feeling any special concern, he developed a dramatic style that no longer touched the reader inwardly but, rather, almost as though in a theater, ushered him into the spectator's seat, where he could watch with detachment the confusing antics of innumerable actors of every temperament and disposition. In order to make these demonstrations more

vivid, it can be said that the dramatic dialogue technique of
story telling, which Heinrich Mann developed for himself as
an author, is the exact opposite of Bert Brecht's "epic theater." Mann's technique aimed at creating an illusion, while
Brecht's would demand critical reflection even while the play
was in progress in this manner. Brecht later on freed himself
as an author from the technique familiar to him as a reader
and spectator.

In an autobiographical letter written in 1943, Heinrich
Mann described the fifteen-year period between the turn of
the century and the outbreak of the First World War by
saying that, during that time, he had achieved only "literary"
success. [38] The limiting word "only" gives us pause. It is
worthwhile at this point to inquire just what was understood
by "literary" success, and why the writer was not content
with it. When we are curious about the success of an author,
an examination of the size of published editions usually provides the most convenient measurement. According to the
data in the German Book Catalog for the years in question,
the six novels of the artistic period (*Im Schlaraffenland,*
1901; *Die Göttinnen,* 1902; *Die Jagd nach Liebe,* 1903; *Professor Unrat,* 1905; *Zwischen den Rassen,* 1907; *Die kleine
Stadt,* 1909) were published by Albert Langen, Paul Cassirer,
and Anton Kippenberg (Insel Verlag) in the usual first editions of "more demanding" authors of 4,000 copies each. We
can determine only indirectly if these copies were ever sold.
Heinrich Mann himself later expressed a very skeptical opinion, while Herbert Ihering felt that the frequent changes of
publisher were responsible for the small sales. [39] Until the
sudden success of *Der Untertan,* Mann had certainly not
made any publisher especially happy. Yet we may surmise
from the fact that a one-volume edition of the expensive
three-volume novel *Die Göttinnen* was published that, though
sales were going rather slowly and needed additional pro-
motion, demand was ultimately sufficient to empty the

storeroom. The last novel to be published before the war, *Die kleine Stadt,* ran to four editions in a short time, thus showing that Heinrich Mann had won a somewhat wider public, even if he was still discontented with the public success of this book.[40]

The publishing house of Kurt Wolff took over the entire corpus of Mann's work during 1917 and 1918. For this period conditions are easier to interpret. Among the author's previously published works, the one time minor sensation, *Im Schlaraffenland,* soon took the lead with a sale of over 60,000 copies. The remaining novels followed with between 15,000 and 45,000 copies printed and probably sold. Relatively small was the printing of *Professor Unrat,* which, before it became famous through the film version, traded at the rear of the artistic novels with a printing of only slightly over 10,000 copies. The unpredictability of successful sales is also shown in the case of the first two volumes of *Die Kaiserreich-Trilogie,* which were also published by Wolff as Mann's then latest works. The second volume, *Die Armen,* was published first. As the political pendulum in Germany was swinging to the left at that time, the publisher risked an initial printing of 50,000 copies, which were actually printed and sold since another edition of 15,000 copies followed shortly thereafter. *Der Untertan* had appeared, almost in its entirety, in a Munich magazine that had suddenly dropped the story in a burst of voluntary patriotic fervor due to the outbreak of the war. This fact made the publisher more wary, and, in 1918 he authorized a first printing of only 7,000 copies. His astonishment can well be imagined when about 150,000 copies of this novel were sold almost at once.

In the twenties, after yet another change of publisher to Paul Zsolnay, the reputation of Heinrich Mann already justified a first printing of 20,000 or 30,000 copies of his novels, although the last book published before his emigration, *Ein ernstes Leben* (1932), fell back to a first printing of only

12,000 copies. It is also worthy of note that, after *Der Untertan,* only *Im Schlaraffenland* in 1929 reached a printing of 100,000 copies under the auspices of the Deutsche Buchgemeinschaft. "Ullstein-AG" brought out, likewise, a pocket edition of *Professor Unrat* in 1930 as an accompaniment to the film, *Der blaue Engel,* and Zsolnay, in publishing Mann's collected works after 1925—an endeavor which certainly depended upon finding readers with a special interest in the author—proceeded cautiously with a printing of only 5,000 copies per volume of the earlier novels. These are the main features of the author's image, changing from decade to decade, insofar as they can be traced through statistics.

Im Schlaraffenland (1901) secured Heinrich Mann's recognition as an author. He thus became an accepted member of the literary world, whose course of development both critics and public were obliged to follow. A Munich epilogue to this Berlin novel was supplied by *Die Jagd nach Liebe* (1903), a book which, due probably to the favorable reception of its predecessor, presumably owes its origin to the wish of the publisher, Langen, although upon Mann's request it was published after *Die Göttinnen,* in order not to nail him to a cliché. Apparently, however, people in Munich had more sensitive nerves than they had in Berlin. The critics took notice of the book primarily in the form of protest, without paying any attention to the strictly "literary" problems, which were admittedly very much overshadowed by the more obvious attractions of the novel.

Another fate befell the monumental *Die Göttinnen.* Although its audacity had made the book controversial from the beginning, the critics greeted it with a certain relief. Finally, it seemed that a comfortable cliché, a legend, or a "message" had been found to which this new talent could be attached. The "Roman" Heinrich Mann could now be profoundly contrasted with his "primeval German" brother Thomas, and this contrast could be based upon Heinrich's long stay in Italy. But Heinrich Mann fought bitterly against any attempt to depict him as a disciple of Gabriele D'Annunzio, [41] and, shortly thereafter, he provided *Professor Unrat* as a refutation of this thesis. It is interesting to note, however, that this novel found almost no critical reaction. Outside of a few critics who knew Mann personally, reviews in the daily press were cool. The initial failure of this book, which was to become so famous later on, cannot therefore be deduced from its author's "un-German" attitude but rather primarily from the fact that it represented an affront to the critics. The same reviewers who would have been ready at any time to hail the passionate "Roman" must have thought it baffling and annoying when an author could take up arms in this fashion against his own established reputation.

With the title *Zwischen den Rassen* Mann tried to make his divided nature clear to the public. He was not concerned here with a reference to his personal consanguine heritage, but rather—as a short autobiography in the Langen catalogue of 1904 proves—with a reference to the experience of his own self, strengthened by travel and residence abroad, and to his feeling of isolation between peoples, classes, and races. [42] But this declaration gained little sympathy for the author in Germany, where nationalism was still so new that people could scarcely get enough of it.

According to the data presented, the characteristics of Mann's "literary" success may be summed up as a lively, although not always favorable, interest of the critics in his work and a small circle of readers whose demands remained constant. If the author, in the letter quoted previously, called the years around 1905 his "happiest" time, we must then assume that he enjoyed his literary success to the fullest at the very moment when it was part of his immediate experience. With his success, it became possible for Heinrich Mann to celebrate publicly that worship of a beauty forbidden to everyday life which Wellkamp of *In einer Familie* had still been obliged to carry on in secret. Thus, Zumsee of *Im Schlaraffenland,* Marehn of *Die Jagd nach Liebe,* and the Duchess of Assy of *Die Göttinnen* became models of the type of wastrels that fixed the canon of "high class" literature. Even *Professor Unrat* treated the same theme, although in a satirical manner. Wasn't the scholar of ancient philology, who preached the will to power and fell victim to the lures of a cheap music hall draped in the national colors, and who finally led solid citizens into the land beyond good and evil, was he not simply Nietzsche under the spell of Wagner? [43] This conclusion can also be reached by observing that, in contrast to current opinion, the figure of the German professor was enthusiastically welcomed by later radical right-wing criticism,[44] while Mann's heroes were obviously the provocative student, Lohmann, and the provoking show girl, Fröhlich. The intoxication of this newly won artistic freedom seemed to extend so far that Thomas Mann thought it necessary to warn his brother: "You know, I believe, that you have gone to the other extreme in that you are now nothing more than an artist. But a poet—God help me—has to be more than just an artist."[45]

The contrast made here between artist and poet is characteristic of the social rise and literary devaluation of the status of writing as a profession from the standpoint of the bourgeois public in the late nineteenth and early twentieth centuries.[46] "Poet" (French *poète,* German *Dichter*) was the older designation for the creative writer. From him, as Thomas Mann pointed out, the bourgeois public expected more than "pure" art. The poet was the last resort any professedly "individual" person could turn to. Whatever he brought along in education, enlightenment, edification, shock, entertainment, experience of life, and firmness of principle was more trustworthy than all other knowledge, even though it might be more systematic and more consistent with logical thinking. Such a dependence of the public on the writer did not, in general, exclude a critical instinct for the immediate value of an individual author and for the eternal incongruity of poetry, truth, and reality. The essence of the relationship between author and reader in the bourgeois world, however, could not be determined by factual questions as to the verisimilitude, correctness, and aesthetic value of his work but rather, above all, by inquiry about that trustworthiness. A basic change in this relationship occurred as a result of the rise of the "artist" (French *artiste,* German *Künstler*). The poet lived the borrowed life of a favorite of the nobility, although this existence was often quite acceptable in material terms. Yet, in his work, he freely bore witness to the bourgeois style of life so clearly different from his own. In other words, he subordinated his life to his work.

The poet wanted to serve his public, the artist to dominate it. But since, in this context, domination was manifested in the right of the artist to give way arbitrarily to whatever caprice might strike his fancy, the artist's most important task was the destruction of any trustworthy relation between reader and author. The reader had to be shocked, by formal and anti-moral experiments, into total confusion. He must never be sure just what his new master had in mind for him. The growing wealth of the bourgeoisie furthered these tyrannical demands of "art" by increasing the number of men of letters as well as the moral flippancy of the public, which to be sure, did not read the "artist" but were at least willing to tolerate his antics. Around the turn of the century, the existence of a writer thus became for the first time in Western cultural history a life style in its own right. As his literary work served exclusively as proof of this fact, the author of that era finally managed to bridge the former gulf between a despised life and a highly valued work. The reevaluation of values was complete.

Mann's concept of the social function of literature did not, however, come to fulfillment in the motif of aesthetic extravagance but rather took it as a challenge. The highest principle of the canon of extravagance was heedless performance. Yet, for Heinrich Mann, even in his wildest creative moods, always persisted some remnants of the moral scruples of a bourgeois reader. The aristocracy of wealth of *Im Schlaraffenland* and of *Die Jagd nach Liebe,* as well as the aristocracy of birth of *Die Göttinnen* and of *Zwischen den Rassen,* paid homage in one form or another to the principle of performance, while, for the heroes of the artistic novels, touched by bourgeois influence, contemplation tasted sweeter than action. The rather sultry chastity of their love affairs may be seen as an exemplary expression of constantly restrained action. Also, in its general layout, a monumental work like *Die Göttinnen* is more convincing because of its abundance in intellectual and emotional highlights, inaccessible to the average person, rather than because of the consistency of its narrative plot and outline.

The neglect of action in favor of sentiment, of living in favor of passive experience, often brought Mann in those days the reputation of being a skillful hack. With this excuse, both critics and public could protect themselves from the acknowledgment of the somewhat embarrassing recognition that Heinrich Mann belonged completely neither to the poets nor to the artists, that he could not be placed either with the aristocrats or with the bourgeois, and could not be numbered either among the libertines or among the philistines. He was, rather, an offense to both sides. His divided position was perhaps most clearly defined by the large element of satire hidden in all of the novels of his artistic period and directed at both camps. When—in his essay on Flaubert—Mann explained, "No one has ever written good satire without having some sort of affinity to what he held up to ridicule. He is either an apostate or one who has been shut out. In satire there is envy or disgust, but always an outraged sense of community. No stranger will succeed in it," [47] he was describing his own position at the time. To the public that had borne him and with whose eyes he had always read books, he was an apostate. To the public of his choice, for whom he intended to write books, he was still an outsider whose mimicry was a source of shame.

Heinrich Mann's novel *Die kleine Stadt,* which he himself considered a turning point in his work when it appeared in 1909, was supposed to end the period of mere "literary" success. The artistic period had begun with the shoulder-shrugging resignation of an author who had "no people in common with me." It ended with the "burning desire" of the composer Dorlenghi "to compose music for an entire nation."[48] The relationships to society that Mann described in a rather stylized manner here must not be taken too literally. In the period of his literary success Heinrich Mann, assisted by liberal criticism, had gained a reputation with the metropolitan public on which he was later able to rely. His word would be worth something because during his literary period he had become an established writer.

But this reputation was, in his opinion, not equivalent to the social function of literature. If Nietzsche had turned from Wagner to Bizet, it was, according to one of Mann's earlier statements, because he preferred the work of the Frenchman as an example of "national artistic unity" over Bayreuth, which had become a playground for international snobbery.[49] Mann's own longtime residence abroad, which had actually made him a citizen of the world, had not been able to erase his natural sensitivity for the linguistic nationality of literature. Thus, he admired how Mascagni's veristic opera, *Le Maschere,* had succeeded, by presenting only masks, "each from one of the hundred cities of Italy, each a traditional character," to depict a sum total of "humanity," i.e., the entire population of the country.[50] A merely literary success certainly brought with itself a respectable social position for the author, but only with a public that took particular

interest in literary subjects. In order to win fame as a national
poet, an author had to seek the applause of those who had
been ruthlessly expelled from the inner circle of art or who
had originally been remote from literary activity in general.
His latest book described the revival of national sentiments,
even though its action was unobtrusively set in a small Italian
city of the mid-nineteenth century.

The "humanity" of *Die kleine Stadt* was divided quite
simply. In the boxes of the municipal theater sat the gentry:
a baron, a rich merchant, a landowner, a government official.
The balcony was filled with self-employed craftsmen and
petit bourgeois, while the pit contained the common people:
servants, maids, clerks, apprentices, a few respectable tarts,
and some well-known local eccentrics. Political life was limited
to the intermediary role between the social classes, played by
a lawyer as the man of social progress and the town secretary
as the representative of political reaction. For the reader of
1909, little progress of any kind was to be seen. The small
town read by candlelight, rode on the mail coach, and
worked at home or in the fields. Politics was purely local in
the sense of the magazine article by Mann quoted earlier. The
enmities of the province centered around an "old bucket,"
won in a campaign years ago, which the local clergyman kept
hidden from public view in the belfry, much to the anger of
the local progressives. The "humanity" of *Die kleine Stadt*
was, to a great extent, economically independent, politically
unaffiliated, and its historic memories extended no farther
than Garibaldi and the election of the last pope. This is how
the population of the small Italian town stood before the
reader: affable without clinging to any liberal dogma, God-
fearing but still glad to hear a coarse jest about wandering
nuns, patriotic but not forgetting that the state they lived in
had been created by their own fathers and brothers. Vast
economic conflicts and political intrigues, no longer comprehensible to the individual, were unfamiliar to them, as were

those social upheavals that, like the French Revolution, had spread outward from the large cities. Nowhere did Mann's novel state clearly whether the small town was part of a monarchy or a republic. Even the severe motif of *The Marriage of Figaro,* as used in *Die arme Tonietta,*[51] an opera performed in the novel, lost some of its sinister power in that the participants, despite barriers of class distinction, met one another practically on a first name basis.

Only on the far horizon a faint glimmer could be detected of the social process that Heinrich Mann wanted to exemplify in the theatrical uproar: the birth of the nation state, depicted here as the result of the performance of an opera by a group of artists, which led the people to discover their own unity. The ideal of "humanity" coming to national consciousness, however, never appeared on the scale that had terrified Goethe at Valmy, but rather always in idyllic miniature. The irritation with which Mann reacted to criticism on this point is easy to understand.[52] As soon as he tried to reach beyond mere literary success for the applause of the general public, it was important for him to touch properly in dimension on the geographical and sociopolitical ideas of his time. In the year 1909, however, the split between his polished, thoroughly modern literary language and the old-fashioned political and moral ideals he praised in that language had become so deep that the wider public, which he sought and which understood a novel primarily in terms of its content, could hardly think of him as a writer in touch with the times. The artist in Heinrich Mann had fully accepted the freedoms granted him by his contemporaries. But the poet in him still clung to the "classic" concept of the social function of literature, which he had drawn from prerevolutionary writers.

The motif of the theater appeared in *Die kleine Stadt,* just as it had in *Im Schlaraffenland.* Here, however, it was enlarged to an extensive correspondence between the action of

the depicting and the depicted art work. Above all, the
ending of the novel and the ending of the opera performed
therein correspond to one another with the clarity of a
parable. Despite this surprising twist, *Die kleine Stadt* is not a
theatrical novel in the usual sense. The author's reserve toward stagecraft showed itself once again in his then latest
work in that, although a "Gesamtkunstwerk" appeared—"one
which a single mind created and which no technician helps to
bring to life" [53]—not a fraction of the care manifested in the
novel was devoted to the aesthetic questions raised by the
performance depicted in it. To the presentation of art by art,
i.e., literature—which, as such, came quite near to being a
vicious circle—was added the refusal to include all those
material details that are expected from a novel about an
opera, the accent being exclusively on the nonartistic effects
of art. This outlook quite naturally led Heinrich Mann to
introduce as an audience for the art work depicted not a
public but the people, not that art work's social environment
but rather an arbitrarily chosen political opposite. Even more
important was the discrepancy that, as an active object of his
depiction, this "folk" possessed an undeniable aesthetic
charm and moved with the grace and smoothness of a ballet
ensemble. But as an observing and creative subject it had
scarcely any artistic or critical capabilities. The audience,
therefore, of *Die arme Tonietta* in *Die kleine Stadt* obviously
needed no experience of the demonic art into which the
performers of the opera had been initiated elsewhere. For the
demands of this audience it seemed to suffice that the performers climbed onto some overturned vegetable crates and
proclaimed a few rhetorical commonplaces. The task of the
opera performers, so far as the audience was concerned, consisted in communicating convictions rather than accomplishments. The understanding of accomplishments would have
required a corresponding ability. Convictions were accessible
without such an ability through mere goodwill.

Even at the level of the art work depicted, Heinrich Mann distinguished sharply between art, as demonstrated in the relationship between the composer Dorlenghi and his chief performer, and rhetoric, as shown in the relationship between performers and audience. Rhetoric, on the other hand, was given little free play. To be sure, Heinrich Mann felt no fear of the celebration of tumultuous action in which all distance between art and life, stage and audience, play and earnest was temporarily removed. Yet he carefully limited the political results of the rhetoric to the area of a small provincial town that might be permitted to go through one night of public commotion, only to sink back into its rustic torpor the following morning. Furthermore, the opera performance certainly brought about that idyllic communal experience of "humanity" in the small town that allowed the composer Dorlenghi, despite his temporary despair over the chaotic conditions in the theater, to be satisfied with his audience, as: "The singing shapes were stronger and purer than they were, and yet identical with them. Then they were happy to be men. They loved one another." [54] Yet the total political and social situation of the town remained practically the same, before and after the idolized theatrical revolution, despite the fears of the "gentlemen" that an uproar was developing with the middle class against the nobility and the poor against the rich.[55]

The real "Gesamtkunstwerk" of *Die kleine Stadt* was not on the level of the opera presented but on that of the novel itself. If it is agreed that since the Enlightenment, the novel, through the engagement of the reader, had won the social function which, up to that time, had been fulfilled by the sermon, [56] then it can also correctly be asserted that, with *Die kleine Stadt,* Heinrich Mann had freed himself formally and completely from the traditional concept of literature he had acquired as a reader. In this novel, he overcame completely the former bourgeois emphasis on subject matter in

literature. "The confusing analyses which made of the old
novel a blend of adventure and essay are done away with, and
with them the entire exposition, since the author never
speaks in his own name any more, and everything that he
once provided as an introduction now splinters in the course
of the game into sensations and springs with a life of its own
from his creations. The method serves perfectly here for the
first time." [57] Flaubert, for whom Mann's remarkably strik-
ing description was valid, had already deprived the reader of
his role as engaged participant and relegated him to the position of a mere onlooker. Instead of encountering suggestions,
decisions, arguments, questions, contradictions, consolation,
and counsel as previously, thereby feeling the world of the
novel raised to a reality that was more than just paper, the
reader of *Madame Bovary* saw this reality banished from the
pages of a book again through the technique of the illusionist
novel. Thus, books once an almost tedious but indispensable
means for the establishment of contact between author and
reader, had actually become their own purpose and also, in
doing so, a purpose without purpose beyond. Communication no longer took place between author and reader through
books, but between readers and books that suddenly seemed
to have an existence independent of their authors.

   Die kleine Stadt represented the completion of this development insofar as it made the objectified relationship between
art and its public itself again the object of depiction. The separation of the aesthetic and the rhetorical circuits made the
reader of the novel a disinterested observer of observers who
were themselves not immediately participating in art. The
book might attempt a vague political statement but could not
take on a new social function, because of the double barrier
of narrative technique that it had raised between itself and its
reader. Using this novel as an example, it can be shown quite
clearly that the decision to adopt a definite literary technique
is identical with the author's understanding of himself, i.e.,

with his concept as reader of the social role, social status, and social function of the author.

After having followed the canon of aesthetic extravagance—in the five predecessors to *Die kleine Stadt*—so often and so purely that he already felt like having taken on the role of a "pariah of the elite," who looked into the distance for the "new state" in which he might once again be a citizen, [58] Heinrich Mann returned with his latest book to the pedagogical lowlands. Yet the echo of his appeal to "humanity" was apparently so slight in the ears of the author that, in his disappointment, he felt obliged to speak of a "fiasco." [59] Generally though, the reviews of the book were quite favorable, and even the superpatriot journal *Der Kunstwart* contented itself with the remark that it would have been preferable for a German author to write a novel about a German small town rather than to present a wretchedly amateurish picture of Italy. [60] Mann's dissatisfaction with the impression left by the novel can therefore only lead to the conclusion that his manifesto directed to all mankind had been perceived merely as an aesthetic embellishment, because, as a result of the objectifying technique of the book, scarcely any of its readers could have supposed that the "humanity" about whom the novel spoke was also that to whom it spoke.

As Heinrich Mann had freed himself from the traditional formal concept of literature, readers of *Die kleine Stadt* could no longer discover Heinrich Mann the reader in the language of the novel and determine their attitude on his. Mann the reader was easily detectable in the content of the novel, but his attitude certainly appeared old-fashioned in the eyes of his contemporaries. Thus, it was perhaps the discrepancy between matter and form, between formal liberties taken by the author and the material limitations of Heinrich Mann the reader, that prevented the book from gaining a significant reputation.

The "humanity" so often invoked in *Die kleine Stadt* was also, more generally considered, not the public of the writer but rather his court of appeal, and only possibly the literary model of his readership as well. Speaking more exactly, this "humanity" had once actually been the model of the bourgeois public when this public still felt the need of calling on "humanity" for assistance in various political undertakings. In the year 1909, however, the bourgeois public no longer needed any "nonsense about humanity" (a term used by the late Kaiser Wilhelm). Disregarding this fact, it is obvious that the court of appeal for a writer who really wrote for the whole human race of our planet and the literary model of this very "humanity" could well be two quite different phenomena.

In a remarkable fashion, the distance between the man of letters and his public asserted itself just at the moment when Heinrich Mann had the least desire for it. In the eighteenth and early nineteenth centuries, this distance had resulted from the social career of the writer. Following the example of numerous predecessors, he left the bourgeois public as a person, but remained inseparably united with it as a writer. After the bourgeois revolution, the possibility of social advancement for the author as a person disappeared. Now he could maintain his distance from the public only by stressing the inaccessibility of his work. As every potential new author became acquainted with literature as a bourgeois reader under this aspect, his highest ambition as a writer became to renew this distance from the public.

Heinrich Mann's path from the role of bourgeois reader to that of bourgeois author had repeated this sociohistorical development on a biographical scale. In addition to gaining his freedom as an artist, he was even permitted, in *Die kleine Stadt,* to make a public speech on political matters—an opportunity which would certainly have aroused the envy of his eighteenth-century colleague. Yet, even though it would have been impossible for this colleague to cry in one of his novels, "humanity will always have new masters to overthrow, and spirit will always have to struggle with power,"[61] Heinrich Mann, nonetheless, stood outside of the public to whom he turned. The objectifying technique of his novel proved that he felt himself somehow obligated to the public, but not united with it as an equal member. Readership was the object and aim of his work but not its controlling factor. The readers of *Die kleine Stadt* certainly received political arguments but no instruments of social communication. The chance, therefore, for the writer Heinrich Mann, now at the pinnacle of his creative development, to escape once again from the confines of mere literary success and adulation consisted primarily in gaining the interest of a sector of the political public to whom literature might be more important as an argument than as a communicative instrument.

2 The Shadow of Legend (1910-1925)

Die Kaiserreich-Trilogie, Diktatur der Vernunft

IN 1941, Heinrich Mann, discussing the origin of his *Kaiserreich-Trilogie,* said: "I began assembling the material for a novel of the bourgeois German under the regime of Wilhelm II *(Der Untertan)* in 1906. I finished the manuscript in 1914, two months before the War broke out. . . . The novel of the Proletariat, called *Die Armen,* was finished during the War in 1916. I only began to deal with the leading figures of the Empire in the Summer of 1918, a few months before the collapse. . . . In the first draft of *Der Kopf,* I still found it advisable to situate the action in a country with a fictitious name."[1]

Perhaps it is not without significance that Mann conceived the plan for the story of the loyal subject Hessling, whose career was furthered particularly by his ability to imitate the mannerisms and rhetoric of the Kaiser, in that very year when the cobbler Wilhelm Vogt, from Köpenick, later on the hero of Carl Zuckmayer's famous drama, succeeded with his ingenious practical joke.

The correct analysis of the trilogy demands above all that we separate the original intentions of the author from its later reputation. Strange as it may seem, the origins of *Der Untertan* reached back into the eighteenth century, for the conflict of conscience mentioned previously that comes to light again in this book had its roots in the social configurations of that time. This conflict sprang from the double obligation of the bourgeois writer: his social obligation to the people, i.e., to his newly won bourgeois public, and his literary obligation to the world of the spirit, i.e., the values of the literary tradition of which he was going to become a part. The bourgeois writer took the task of aiding the new public in reaching social self-consciousness quite seriously. But he was equally anxious not to "throw into the clumsy hands of the bourgeoisie"[2] the treasures of the spirit. Socially dependent on a noble patron as a person, and witnessing a foreign, i.e., the bourgeois, way of life as an author, he found these treasures of the spirit to be his only real possession. Author and critics reassured one another constantly of the inadequate literary and aesthetic appreciation of the populace, that is, their readers. Thus, even before the advent of the notorious artist with his esoteric way of life, the "famous" writer of the eighteenth century had gradually given way to the "misunderstood" poet as their "missing link" insofar as it was constantly intimated to the public that it could never do justice to the poet's literary qualities. The words of the French skeptic Chamfort, who noted that fame gives a person the advantage of being known to all those who do not know him or her personally, adopted, in addition to their original social significance, a figurative "literary" meaning, according to which the best known author was always the one most difficult to appreciate.

The literary career of an author was more or less laid out on a straight line, running between the social function of literature as the starting point and its independent aesthetic value as the goal. This line was the path by which the author made his way from traditional bourgeois morality to traditional literary aesthetics. The self-assuredness of the writer sprang from the very awareness that his person provided the only juncture between these two spheres. His aloofness from the public within the framework of the artistic conception of literature betrayed, therefore, something of the conceit of the specialist who jealously guarded his secrets, without forgetting, however, that he owed his training and his sustenance to an indispensable circle of patrons. This patronage even expected of him at least enough unbourgeois mumbo-jumbo to make them feel sure they were not giving attention and support to someone not worth it. Viewed objectively, the freedom of the artist and the poet is therefore essentially the same as that enjoyed by other specialists in the human community, as for instance, the doctor, to whom no patient can prescribe what he is to do in order to heal him. On the other hand, even the physician usually needs the consent of the patient for the treatment he plans—a gesture that the artistic writer thought he could dispense with in the case of his bourgeois public.

Heinrich Mann's development from reader to author in the early days of his life as a writer had been nothing less than a demonstration of his "worthiness." This development proceeded from the clever manipulation of skeptical and prophetic intentions of *In einer Familie* to the radical separation of aesthetics and rhetoric of *Die kleine Stadt.* In *Der Untertan* he once again used the technique of avoiding the burgher on aesthetic territory in favor of a retreat to the specialist's realm, while remaining the ally of the bourgeoisie in social disputes. In contrast to *Die kleine Stadt,* where the playful style had prevented a strong engagement of the reader, *Der Untertan* regained this engagement by its bold satirical color. If Köpf of *Im Schlaraffenland,* in immediate adoption of the concept of the aesthetically better educated specialist, had already complained about the German people—"whom not even some good honest hiding could move to pick up a book"[3]—then the education of the loyal subject, Diederich Hessling, was designed to serve as proof of this very thesis. At school, the German composition and anyone who did well in it were strange and suspicious to him. At home, his father watched carefully, lest his mother spoil him by letting him read novels in secret. Later, the product of this education prided himself on having hocked his Schiller at the first favorable opportunity and led his beloved to the window of a butcher shop, where he declared that this sight took the place of any enjoyment of art with him.[4] Even Hessling's later position as a paper manufacturer was an obvious irony: The prosaic burgher as creator of the raw material of literature confronted fully on purpose with Mann, the artistic writer, as creator of just this philistine figure, in whose eyes that writer's activity could only consist in the waste of costly material for useless scribblings. If Heinrich Mann saw his literary relation to the burgher Hessling this way, then it was only a natural result that, at about the same time when the author let his still unpublished "loyal subject" proclaim that the novel was no "German art," a critic, without any personal antipathy, should call Heinrich Mann "the most repellent of all German novelists for the average reader."[5] The relation between author and public hinted at here was even more distinctly outlined by the fact that, in the novel, the opponents of Hessling, viz., old Buck and his son, had to appear not only as burghers but also as artists, albeit of a rather amateurish sort. They were, therefore, not confronted with the problem of appreciating art, as was Hessling. On the contrary, they were permitted to regard this philistine with the same condescension as their creator.

That Heinrich Mann remained true to both the aesthetic as well as the social function of bourgeois literature is shown in Hessling's attendance at the fictitious playlet *Die heimliche Gräfin* and at the opera *Lohengrin,* by Richard Wagner. The homecooked production by the wife of an undersecretary who belonged to the old Prussian nobility and the work of a great composer filled Hessling with the same naive enthusiasm. His hopeless failure when confronted with any aesthetic experience shows that Heinrich Mann considered him as being incapable in this area by his very nature. But while the skeptical aesthete in Mann the writer demonstrated brilliantly in this fashion his allegedly homeless situation amidst a public living absolutely insensitive to any literary values whatever, the political moralist in Heinrich Mann neither saw himself as homeless nor thought his readers unteachable. To be sure, Hessling accepted without reservation that the playlet of Frau von Wulckow ridiculed the "rude manners" of the bourgeoisie—although the "better manners" of her noble husband also left something to be desired.[6] Hessling certainly honored Wagner's "national" art because its author "placed the highest value on nobility and on God's favor."[7] In general, however, the satire here rang more of sermonizing and appeals to moral conscience than of resigned aloofness from the public. The opportunism and chicanery of the bourgeoisie by no means prevented Heinrich Mann from believing in a better future for that class. On the contrary, those defects challenged the moralist in him to make that future a reality.

This task had not yet been achieved because the German bourgeoisie, unlike the middle classes of other western European countries, had not succeeded, during the course of its social rise, in making its political rights correspondingly secure. One difficulty arose from the financial dependence of the majority of the bourgeoisie, as public officials, on the individual states of the German empire.[8] Nonetheless, Hessling's sarcastic verdict on the elder Buck, "Sentenced to death in '48"—sarcastic insofar as the old liberal had actually been sentenced to death as a rebel, but later on pardoned—marked him as well as his more likable counterparts. For all three of them, although claiming to be activists each in his kind, had undertaken very little in the area of politics. Bismarck's "social laws" were the work of a member of the nobility and thus preempted the German bourgeoisie of a task which, in other western European countries, justified before the people the right to rule. Without this proof of political effectiveness and responsibility, the German bourgeoisie remained dependent upon the authorities and intimidated by the presence of a people that those authorities could play off against them at any time.

As the German bourgeoisie had scarcely made use of the opportunities offered by its position as Third Estate between the political fronts of the nobility and the people, Heinrich Mann was almost haunted by the evident idea that its right to political rule could be established through a spectacular intellectual and literary achievement. As a result, Mann, at the same time that he was drawing the unflattering portrait of the bourgeois German under the rule of Wilhelm II, also, in his article "Reichstag," published in *Pan*,[9] summoned these bourgeois Germans to a new national convention. Accordingly, in his trial for insulting the Kaiser, as depicted in *Der Untertan*, even Hessling stood before the bar of justice not as a convicted criminal but rather as a clumsy witness on behalf of the bourgeoisie. Also, when the lawyer for the inconsiderate manufacturer Lauer, who had invoked the Imperial House against the cause of the bourgeoisie,[10] demanded in his plea the "awakening of the burgher" as the "truly national deed," he was directing his exhortations to the witness Hessling as well. In order to sum up the moral and political intentions of the first part of *Die Kaiserreich-Trilogie*, it can be said that at the time of the action of the novel (about 1890) as well as at that of its writing (about 1910) it was "by no means too late for the Hesslings to search their souls."[11] Of course, it remains an open question whether or not Mann, with such "classic" ideas of the function of the man of letters in bourgeois society, lagged far behind the actual relations of his time, as he had already in *Die kleine Stadt*.

The later reputation of *Der Untertan* was based on a broad public echo, which Heinrich Mann had helped to prepare. After the fiasco of the friendly fable of the inhabitants

of the Italian small town, Mann agreed to the printing of
excerpts from the far more bitter tasting tale of the German
provincials in the magazines *Simplizissimus* and *März* and,
finally, even before the completion of the manuscript, to an
unabridged advance publication in the magazine *Zeit im Bild*
in Munich. In addition, the success of the intended edition in
book form was aided still more by the fact that the author,
through his recent contributions to various newly established
literary periodicals, like *Die Aktion, Pan, Das Forum, März,
Die weissen Blätter,* and others, had once again involved himself more deeply in the cultural and political debates of the
day. Like the Nietzsche of 1880, Heinrich Mann at forty had
matured around 1910 into a literary model, and his appearance in these journals was especially welcomed by the younger
generation of editors, who thereby obtained unexpected support for their literary programs from a recognized literary
authority. Above all, Heinrich Mann's invocation of the
"spirit" in *Die kleine Stadt,* as well as in two essays related to
that novel, "Geist und Tat" and "Der französische Geist," of
1910, seemed to have fascinated those ambitious sons of the
bourgeoisie. The articles, stories, and poems of those young
writers attacked everything: the imperial family and Social
Democracy, press and censorship, the army and the pacifist
societies, profit hunting and outmoded tax laws, business
management and labor unions. A curious blend of political liberalism and cultural conservatism was carried to its most radical exaggeration. Compulsive anarchism demanding action at
any price was joined to esoteric ideas of a "global empire of
the spirit."[12]

Der Untertan was soon drawn into this whirlpool of writings plagued with chiliasm. To be sure, Hessling was originally
intended merely to take his place in the gallery of caricatures
of Prussian splendor, Teutonic braggadocio, tasteless display
of wealth, and social obsequiousness so familiar to the
readers of a popular illustrated magazine.[13] Yet, scarcely had

the first chapters been published, when the activist chorus made itself heard. Apparently, members of this chorus thought they aided the latest work of the honored master best by confirming that "by chance" it possessed the gift of being able to evoke extraliterary effects of the "spirit." "If, after reading *Werther,* people shoot themselves, the book is good. If they shoot others, then it is even better."[14]

Four months after this provocative statement, the war began, which *Der Untertan* had to enter evidently with considerable political ballast. The fate of the book, however, would not depend on its "catastrophic" conclusion—which became so famous only later on but was still lacking in the advance publication, halted at the outbreak of the war and known only to the author.[15] When Heinrich Mann required, therefore, that the editor of the magazine refrain from any comment on the interruption of the novel's publication,[16] it was not only because he wished to have a free hand with the text, but also because he wanted to control the reputation of the whole work. When the shots—which the young activists had so longingly desired—started to strike bourgeois Germans under the reign of Wilhelm II, not only the conclusion (Hessling is caught in a downpour at the dedication of a monument to the Kaiser) but the entire novel lost its meaning as a moral preachment to a bourgeoisie neglectful of its political obligations. Malignant critics might interpret the shots fired by foreign enemies at the German bourgeoisie as the secret wish of the author, for, without any idea of how soon his visions were to become grim reality, Heinrich Mann had praised the "singing hills of Valmy" and the French "soldiers of reason" in essays published shortly before *Der Untertan.*[17] Although originally intended as a parable to be applied to internal politics, a great part of Heinrich Mann's recently completed work was subtly changing into dangerous commentary on foreign policy.

Objectively speaking, the success of *Der Untertan* depended on a German defeat. A victory would probably have sealed the fate of an apparently defeatist novel that could be labeled as an anti-German pamphlet. In fact, the author, anticipating a possible military defeat, showed unusual political foresight by his removal of the "anti-German" point in the still unpublished manuscript. He did so by asserting that the history of the French bourgeoisie—i.e., in a broader sense the history of the present enemy—had also ended in its downfall. This thesis lies at the core of Heinrich Mann's essay on Zola, which appeared in 1915 and gave the reader a foretaste of the theme of the full-length edition of *Der Untertan.* The essay was, of course, highly questionable from a historical viewpoint, since the war of 1870-1871 could be compared with that of 1914-1918 only in that many soldiers had to die in both. But the invocation of Zola, whom Mann believed to have "predicted" the historical end of the French bourgeoisie in *Les Rougon-Macquarts,* [18] saved Mann's work from being ignored. For only the legend of being the prophet of Germany's downfall could justify the political moralism of *Der Untertan.*

The creation of this legend was an extraordinarily daring self-manipulation of the reputation of Mann's novel, whereby its original message was transformed into almost its complete opposite. The author had converted his appeal for moral reflection and ensuing revolutionary action into resigned acceptance of catastrophic accomplishment. Even if history finally did conform to the prophecies of an unwritten, i.e., unpublished, book, this affirmation of the thesis of *Der Untertan* had the effect of a Pyrrhic victory. The affirmation made the author the prisoner of his own legend, and a rather disappointing legend at that. To be sure, due to the promotional effects provided by the advance publication in the illustrated magazine, due to the clever propaganda of the publisher of the book, due to the critics' approval of the legend, and, last but not least, due to the publicity the author had received from a public quarrel with his brother during the war, *Der Untertan* could be read as a great success by all

those Germans "to whom the lost war had first brought concern over their conditions." [19] Yet the novel could not disguise the fact that it was essentially a prewar book. The
"defeated Germany," looking in *Der Untertan* for the
"prophet of its misfortune," [20] soon discovered that the
book had nothing to say about the decisive experience of the
war, which many of its readers had shared.

The second part of the *Kaiserreich-Trilogie, Die Armen,*
which had been written after *Der Untertan* but was published before, showed the same remarkable shortcoming. The
first part of the trilogy suffered from having neglected to
foresee the only irrevocable historical event of the time.
Heinrich Mann himself explained once with bitter irony: "I
ought to have foreseen [the war], because it was announced in
Der Untertan." [21] In his Zola essay, the writer had later been
obliged to comment on this event and to match the thesis of
his novel to a situation influenced by it. In *Die Armen,* he
would have had the opportunity to write a true novel of the
war and to seek a direct reference to the historical situation.
But when the second part of the trilogy again moved about
the edges of great happenings by making the outbreak of the
war the end of the novel once more, Mann showed just how
much he felt himself a prisoner of that legend which a com-
bination of adverse circumstances concurring at the time of
the publication of *Der Untertan* in the magazine had forced
him to create. A genuine novel of the war, which, written by
an author who had remained at home and now was almost
fifty, did not necessarily have to be a frontline report, could
nonetheless have left the legend of *Der Untertan* behind and
freed Heinrich Mann from bondage to the inaccurate and
burdensome cliché of having been the prophet of Germany's
downfall. But it was not granted to him to write such a book,
since he could place his stakes neither on victory nor on
defeat. To count on victory would have meant sacrificing the
legend at the cost of his personal integrity and literary honor,

without any assurance that this sacrifice would be rewarded. Counting expressly on Germany's defeat would have placed Heinrich Mann in an equally difficult conflict of conscience. When his brother pointed out to him that the proof of the legend would at last establish his literary reputation, Heinrich Mann sadly answered him on January 5, 1918:

> Triumph over what? Over the fact that everything "rests securely," namely the world . . . and ten million dead under the earth? That is indeed a justification! That promises satisfaction to the ideologist! But I am not the man to tailor the misery and death of nations to fit my intellectual idiosyncrasies, not I. I don't believe that victory is even worth talking about when people are dying. Everything that will be gained toward a better humanity, after the final, most frightful things that await us yet, will be bitter and sad.[22]

At the time of the outbreak of the war, Heinrich Mann's bourgeois public had not yet accomplished the revolutionary deed he had urged on in his political Lenten sermon in *Der Untertan*. At first, the author might have believed that a historical verdict on the German bourgeoisie could reinforce his reproach and affirm his remonstrations. In his essay on Zola he had written concerning his novel, "What will be the final outcome of the work? The last word? If it is not collapse, then it has no last word! "[23] In fact, the writer and his derelict public could look one another in the eye once again only if his legend, which had grown in the meantime from a warning to a prognosis, should be actually confirmed.

Just how important the restoration of this mutual trust was to Heinrich Mann was proven by his autobiographical letter to A. Kantorowicz in 1943, in which the author referred to the positive reaction of the public to his drama, *Madame Legros,* [24] which had also been written during the war. In the course of the war, however, Mann realized full of horror that the bourgeois public, for whom *Der Untertan* had summed up the critical balance of their historical past from

as sat in the audience. For the "proletarian" Balrich there existed no distinction between bourgeois art and bourgeois life, and he certainly would not have suspected either that the authors of such art could provoke their public aesthetically or that this public should become excited over their "villainies." To him, both were of the same species, indistinguishable from one another and hence belonged closely together.

In transmitting the legend of *Der Untertan,* which was supposed to deal with the "anticipated" fall of the bourgeois world, to a potential public of workers, Heinrich Mann had to work from a position that was essentially weaker than his previous one. The intellectual gap between poet and proletarian was not the result of a conventional estrangement tolerated by the public but, on the contrary, was based upon an essential objective difference between them. Paradoxically enough, this essential difference would have had to be overcome before the right of the poet to a certain exclusive position could have been reestablished within the framework of a tacitly recognized literary convention.

But Heinrich Mann had also lost much of his former sovereignty in the moral and political area. Since bourgeois literature was "unpolitical," i.e., it stood beyond the political factions of aristocrats and common people, its social function had depended primarily upon a highly refined moral code, of which writers could make use without any consideration of its possible political liabilities. They were concerned only with the repetition of "self-evident" principles before a public already convinced of their validity. As the political opposite of the bourgeoisie, however, the mass of workers could not renounce political representation, so that Heinrich Mann had to calculate from the very start on a verdict, perhaps even a veto, from this powerful group. Actually, he had been waiting, ever since the publication of *Die kleine Stadt,* for the truly political public to show an interest in him and make him a national poet by using his writings as a political argument in the debates of the day.

To his disappointment, however, Social Democrat reviewers rejected *Die Armen* completely. The very same critic who quite comprehensibly accepted *Der Untertan* as an anti-bourgeois pamphlet (but contested the author's right to the legend of his novel with the awkward remark that, *"Before the outburst of his laughter, which was to destroy it, the power already lay in ruins"* [27]) thoroughly condemned *Die Armen*. He also pitied the naiveté occasionally displayed in the plotting, e.g., the idea that the supposed proletarian would carry on his class struggle in the form of a legal battle over an inheritance and, to this end, would occupy himself with Latin and Greek legalisms. [28] He, moreover, rebuked the author for trying to involve the working classes in his literary intentions, thereby pushing himself between them and their legitimate representatives. If Mann's proletarian was somewhat dissatisfied with the party leadership, [29] the party spokesman demonstrated to the writer that it was he who was inwardly remote from the struggles and organizational forms of the proletariat. [30] If Heinrich Mann soberly remarked that social disparities and domestic problems had apparently been casually pushed aside in the national delirium of the war, the literary representative of those "unpatriotic guys" (another famous coinage by the late Kaiser Wilhelm) who had just agreed to the Reich's filling its war chest with bourgeois wealth, would say that the writer was pleading personally for a temporary truce between Balrich and Hessling, falling into sentimental lamentations over the class conflict, and giving way to "unmitigated imperialism." In the light of this reception by the political left, it was no wonder that Heinrich Mann remarked peevishly several years later that:

German Socialists . . . never neglect to point out to me that I,

being bourgeois in origin and way of thinking, am forever cut off
from the proletarian world. Then I can only wish that the proletarian world might find its way to me.[31]

"Will Heinrich Mann care to create a utopia? . . . In revolutions the spirit of utopia is most alive." With these words,
the Social Democrat reviewer of the first two volumes of *Die
Kaiserreich-Trilogie* had closed his critique of *Der Untertan,*
which had finally appeared in book form in 1918. [32] But,
when the third part of the trilogy, *Der Kopf,* a "novel of the
ruling class," appeared in 1925 after seven years of work, not
only the "world collapse" of the war and the storm of the
revolution but also the fantastic frenzy of inflation had
passed over Germany. For a bourgeois writer, born in the
year of a victorious war and the start of an economic rise,
accustomed to being able to live from his inherited income
without depending on the successful sale of his books, there
was, at that time, no reason to create a utopia in anticipation
of the sudden emergence of the best of all possible worlds.
On the contrary, as Mann later wrote in describing the situation of the young postwar writers: "In order for a young
generation to be uniform in spirit, or, to use a nineteenth-
century expression, 'develop itself historically,' one must be
able to believe that its course has a logical basis—something
which ceases to exist as soon as war breaks out." [33] Yet war,
revolution, and an inflation that only a few years later had
eaten up the first larger earnings from the sale of his books
were not reassuring portents for an older writer either.
Marehn, son and heir of a burgher in *Die Jagd nach Liebe,*
had still seen himself in 1903 as "the final result of generations of bourgeois striving toward prosperity, security, and
freedom from illusions," and had therefore prepared himself
for a "completely undisturbed, smooth existence." In *Die
Göttinnen,* which appeared at the same time, the Duchess of
Assy aimed for a life that was only to be "played through,"

like a game with fixed rules. [34] But these rules were suddenly broken, and it became clear just how illusory the idea of a finished world and a reasonably ordered, idyllic life had really become. This meant that in his "Epilogue of the Fallen Empire," Heinrich Mann had to "depict myself, as well as my intellectual generation, along with our disappointed hopes, and our metaphysical yearning, which had never been saturated by real life."[35]

Claudius Terra, the hero of the novel *Der Kopf*, at the beginning and also somewhere in the midst of his checkered career as barker, advertising manager, public defender, Free Conservative delegate in the Reichstag, political advisor to the war industry, then privy councilor and one of the industry's top executives, and finally as secretary of the military court, summarized his political program in the formula: "You can do good business only with the existing social order." [36] Heinrich Mann hàd borrowed this programmatic sentence from his friend Frank Wedekind. It was, however, not meant quite the way it sounded. Actually, Wedekind had, in Mann's opinion, . . . suggested "to recognize the world as it was . . . so that it might swallow and accept the work that was intended to overthrow it."[37]

Terra's goal was also an overthrow of the social order not in the form of organized action by political groups but rather as the act of a single individual. But even this individual surely had no intention of compromising himself by actually taking power. Terra hoped far more for a "spiritual" revolution, for an upheaval that would come about when the hated vocabulary and gesture of contemporary power politics, chauvinism, and imperialism was taken literally, until it had been turned into its opposite. This technique, strongly reminiscent of that employed by certain political comedians, had actually been present in Heinrich Mann's prewar writings, e.g., in those passages of *Der Untertan* in which the attempt was made to surpass even Hessling's byzantinism by the

author and his liberal spokesman calling the Kaiser a "great
artist," and the revolution "a truly national deed," etc. In
Der Kopf, however, Terra was bitterly disappointed by the
Kaiser, who virtually missed all of his cues. This looked as if
the author had known only too well that any hope for success through rhetorical tricks was slim and had just been
interested in finding a justification for a thoroughly imaginary failure. Since, shortly after publication of the novel,
Mann felt it necessary to defend himself against the charge of
having to look for an alibi, [38] it should be noted expressly
that the word justification refers not to Terra's fictious political convictions, but to the supposed failure ascribed to him
and to his creator.

Indeed, Terra's alleged failure takes the reader to the
heart of the matter. The rhetorical technique of the main
figure of *Der Kopf* shows that his creator also pictured himself not as a political leader but rather as a preacher of moral
awakening. Therefore, if in previous chapters, the bourgeois
man of letters has occasionally been called a secularized
cleric, whose revolutionary self-consciousness rested on the
knowledge that his role was neither socially sanctioned nor
properly sanctionable at all, the practical limitations of this
role come to the fore now. The inadequate political activity
of the bourgeoisie assured the preacher that he would scarcely have to compromise himself, but also marked him as a
melancholy clown in the political circus. In his memoirs,
Heinrich Mann also deprecated his own efforts to lead the
"decadent" bourgeois world of 1910 by rhetorical dialectic
back to its age of innocence in about 1850 as quixotic. Yet,
even in *Der Kopf,* he already treated with melancholy irony
Terra's blind faith "to become a rogue for his ideal." Terra
had "lied and betrayed in order to save the world from itself"
and had prided himself on having some sort of *Weltanschauung* throughout his life. "His generation, however, did
not just observe the world, but rather laid it in ruins." [39] At

the end, he admitted ruefully: "I decided to do business with the existing social order. The worst possible thing that could happen has come to pass: I have done so."[40]

The last chapters of the "novel of the rulers," completed almost ten years after the start of the war, stretched almost to the end of the war. The greater the distance from prewar days became, the more condensed the experiences of those days seemed to Mann, so that in *Der Kopf* the policies of wartime Germany were already being formulated by Terra's boyhood friend, Wolf Mangolf, the first bourgeois chancellor of the empire. Terra, the bourgeois intellectual, shared with Mangolf, the bourgeois politician, the blame for having "courted the ruling classes," as Mann had phrased it in his prewar essay.[41] Apparently, they had earned the same reproach as had Hessling. Terra and Mongolf had risen in the service of Prince Lannas in the same way as Hessling had on the coattails of Prefect Von Wulckow. This satire of the prewar bourgeoisie, however, got its point from the fact that the bourgeoisie had not wrested power from the ruling caste: neither Hessling the opportunist, nor Buck the idealist. But Terra the idealist, and Mangolf, the opportunist, became blameworthy in the eyes of the author because they had seized power for themselves in the course of their deals with the Establishment. Terra and Mangolf had merely done, albeit with questionable methods, what their creator had demanded in his politically-oriented prewar works. Each in his own way, they had planned the take-over of power by the bourgeoisie in times of peace and learned instead that their work had led them to the edge of war: one as the wartime chancellor, the other as secretary of the court-martial Germany had been subjected to. The relationship of the two bourgeois figures to the "man in power" was depicted more subtly in *Der Kopf,* however, than in *Der Untertan.* Terra and Mangolf delivered the political power of Prince Lannas into the hands of the industrialist Knack. By this act, they not

only made themselves blameworthy but also became, to a
certain extent, defrauded frauds, since the new "ruling caste"
had no particular advantages at its disposal either. Their lack
of perception, however, justified once again the imaginary
political failure of their creator.

For the author of *Der Untertan,* the prewar world had not
looked bourgeois enough to be worth living in. For the
author of *Der Kopf,* the same prewar world seemed already
too bourgeois to be capable to live on. The first volume of
Die Kaiserreich-Trilogie reached its climax in an assault on a
specific ruling class. The second volume was a pamphlet
against every ruling class. In the first volume, power was a
goal worthy of pursuit. In the third volume, it was the essence of evil. But before jumping to the conclusion that this
condemnation of power is equivalent to that escape from
political responsibility which determined the entire history of
the German bourgeoisie from 1848 to 1914, it must be asked
what may have suggested to Heinrich Mann personally such a
verdict in *Der Kopf.* Since the legend, of having been the
Cassandra of the German bourgeoisie no longer gave the
author complete freedom to admit his own social status as a
bourgeois, the fall of the bourgeoisie was represented in *Der
Kopf* as historically inevitable, because it had become corrupted through the power it had wrested from the old ruling
caste. Due to the legend of *Die Kaiserreich-Trilogie,* it was
part of Heinrich Mann's personal destiny to feel himself so
vulnerable in his relationship to the German bourgeoisie that
he ascribed to that class, in the last part of this work, a
function that, for better or for worse, it had never historically assumed. In the final analysis, the history of the German bourgeoisie had been the story of a social elite, devoid
of any political influence, called on to promote the transition
from an agrarian to an industrial state, only to vanish then
once again politically as an independent Third Estate between rulers and subjects. On the other hand, it was part of

Mann's fate as a writer that he had made this social sacrifice to a very short-lived literary legend. *Der Kopf* was no popular success like *Der Untertan,* it remained a purely literary success. Beyond that point, even those critics who realized something of the supposed "complicity" of Terra failed to comprehend its relationship to the legend of the author.[42]

In 1923, during the inflation, while he was still working on *Der Kopf,* Heinrich Mann published a small volume of collected speeches and essays under the title *Diktatur der Vernunft,* in which he delved into the future of the legend he was carrying with him as he departed from his political period. Before his political period, Heinrich Mann, like the rest of his literary generation, had followed the convention of anti-bourgeois aloofness from the public and thus had faithfully played the role that the late bourgeois public of the turn of the century assigned to the "poetic" writer. Even his entry into the politics of the time with the first volume of *Die Kaiserreich-Trilogie* took place under the aegis of the reputation he had gained by playing this role. Heinrich Mann could take sides in *Der Untertan* because he knew himself surrounded by a public that was struggling to formulate its concept of a "poet," a public that, even if it granted a special position to the "artist," still asked itself constantly just how far his detachment from society might be permitted to go. Hessling's attack on the "un-German" novelist, the critics' assault on the "most repulsive of all German writers," and Mann's own confession of his "personal solitude" in the small autobiography of 1904 by no means bespoke ostracism or an admission of guilt. On the contrary, these statements show the bashful pride of the "poet" in having laid enough obstacles in his path to success to be able to stand as a "master."[43]

But if as a result of his impatience and disillusionment Mann compared the Weimar Republic to the empire in its "hostility to things spiritual,"[44] it was obviously because he

was no longer dealing with a public that felt obliged to respect the "spirit" after having accepted it as an intangible
opposite, but quietly escaped its capture. Suddenly and for
the first time, he was overwhelmed by the frightening sensation that the most important decisions of the time might be
made beyond the bounds of the world of the spirit and,
therefore, also outside the legend to which he had sacrificed
his own class consciousness. Even if this was only a completely subjective and undemonstrable feeling of helplessness
by being exposed to the historical process, it is clear, in any
event, that the concept of literature and creative writing held
by an author over fifty was quite different from that held by
those presumptive groups of readers that had grown to maturity since the war. The aloofness of the author from society
as a social convention of the literary trade, as it had been
practiced around the turn of the century, was not a subject
for debate. This aloofness would have required that the
author had been fully integrated into his public, i.e., as a
person, as well as in regard to his social role as a creative
writer. It was not possible, however, to apply this concept
either to the special case of Heinrich Mann or to writers in
general, since a definite concept of literature and creative
writing had not yet been formulated or accepted by the
potential public. Finally, even if it is assumed that these concepts are to a great extent developed by the author himself, it
must still be asked for what kind of public the author would
have to write. Heinrich Mann began his search for a new
public even as the war was going on and pursued the search
with constant dedication during the years that followed. This
effort indicated also that during those years he was once
again reduced to the role of a trying and questioning reader
and critic than that of a fully developed author.

The "Novel of the Proletarian" had been his first attempt
to find that possible new public. It remained, however, a
polemic, and an unwelcome one at that, since it did not fit

into the official leftist party line. Despite the rejection of his book by Social Democrat critics, and despite the confessed estrangement between the proletarian Balrich and bourgeois art, the writer held fast to his former political standpoint and, in addition, managed to antagonize the "coal mining interests"—in which he saw the "degenerate" successors of the "honest pious small factory owner in his blue apron."[45]
At the beginning of his literary career, Heinrich Mann had accepted a materialist *Weltanschauung* as a legitimate means of perceiving the "substance and direction of all things," provided that the person holding such views was endowed with ample personal wealth and erudition. Yet, in 1923, the same author found a socioeconomic view of history—which made the spiritual restoration of society dependent upon economic progress—totally detrimental to the cause of literature. If even a materialist *Weltanschauung,* in the opinion of the author, required that the possessor of such an ideology have no material problems, then his assertion was, indeed, logically justified also, according to which "the value of an aesthetic work" could be properly appreciated "only by a broad, firmly based, independent middle class."[46] This middle class was not that middle class of Anglo-American origin, i.e., the middle income group of an industrial society, but rather the old Third Estate. If Heinrich Mann's later development led him away from the vicinity of the middle class once again,[47] it was simply perhaps because of the general radicalization of the political vocabulary of the day. Moreover, the concept "middle class" rang in the ears of Mann, the "artist," with certain prosaic overtones of mediocrity. This, however, would only go to prove that, when he made these statements, he still had in mind the old relationship between author and public.

For this reason, there would be little point in seeking from the author a more exact sociological definition of the middle class mentioned above. In 1919, this class was, for

Heinrich Mann, a manifestation of the historical future, a "broad petit bourgeoisie composed of those who labored with head and hands," and one which would rise from the fusion of bourgeoisie and proletariat.[48] In 1923, however, he believed this same middle class to be a part of the historical past and saw in it those previously hidden elements of the bourgeoisie that had been brought to light by the very event that had ruined and almost destroyed them: the inflation.[49]

Vague as these pronouncements may seem as sociological definitions, they were, in a rather odd fashion, quite precise as literary and sociological postulates. For Heinrich Mann the writer, the middle class was quite simply every social level at which the people involved could subscribe to the statement, "We are not rich but very well-to-do," and thus hinted that they were neither materially imperiled nor politically suspect. [50] In the sense of this definition, the bourgeoisie of the eighteenth and early nineteenth centuries was an exemplary German middle class. Far removed from the feudal class struggles between nobles and folk, this Third Estate formed what was, in the best sense, a "revolutionary" public for literature. Sensitive to every sort of literary moralizing, it eagerly waited to be raised as a social group. In this regard, Heinrich Mann could justly point to the model of French history, where the cooperation of "mediocre men" with "revolutionary thinkers" had brought about the events of 1789. [51] At the time of the inflation in 1923, no such middle class was to be found in Germany. The industrial social order embraced both capital and labor, whether as friends or as foes. There was now no Third Estate that would have needed literature as a means of social self-determination, rather than as a political argument, and before which Heinrich Mann could once again have played his well-rehearsed role as a writer.

He felt, however, that men of letters should not simply accept this disturbing knowledge with resignation. If the

"mediocre men" did not find their way to the "moral facts
of life" simply because no one could escape the corrupting
economic and political power struggles of the day, then the
first thrust toward the new rule of the spirit had to come
from the "revolutionary thinker." The writer expressed this
same thought in his novels and essays. In *Der Kopf,* Claudius
Terra wandered through the Tyrolean Alps with a monk be-
longing to a new order not yet recognized by the Church.
The founder of the order, as the monk was able to repoit,
"knows ahead of time what men will do." [52] In the light of
his knowledge of the dubious affairs of the world, his entry
into the cloister was certainly no wonder. But even Terra was
impressed by the Church:

> It is the only form in which the West has seen the spirit trium-
> phant over nonspiritual powers. These powers have smashed
> every other philosophy without exception. The Church has be-
> come a power in itself. "That was the stroke of genius." [53]

With overpowering historical foresight, the Church had asserted itself as the representative of the "spirit" against old
and new "powers."

The Alpine setting of this dialogue shows that Heinrich
Mann was symbolically aiming here at some kind of *Hochland* atmosphere (cf. below, Hochland-Highland). Without
making a direct philosophical commitment, Mann nonetheless was interested in getting a favorable recommendation
from the Catholic press. He had guessed correctly that its
public had come out of the contemporary convulsions
undamaged and relatively uniform in composition and that
he would certainly find that public friendly toward his
praising of the spiritual past. This attempt, which was repeated once again in the novel *Mutter Marie,* was doomed to
failure, however, as the one Catholic literary magazine of
importance, Karl Muth's *Hochland,* was at that time in the

midst of an economic and intellectual crisis. This might well
be taken as symptomatic for the mood of impending doom
felt throughout the literature of the time. The reaction of the
rest of the Catholic press was quite reserved.[54]

But the two characters of the novel were only expressing
what their creator had demanded in his book of essays two
years previously. Confronted with a choice between the
Church and communism, Heinrich Mann, in *Diktatur der
Vernunft,* had decided at once for the Church. Communism,
in the sense of a social evolution, "as Anatole France pro-
claims it," certainly had some good points, but Europe could
not wait until an alteration of its economic forms once again
awakened its "slumbering spirit." Not even the historically
established Catholic church was capable of meeting the needs
of the hour, even though it was "the only organized attempt
of Western society to place its spirit in power and to set it
above all material force." "Who can help? Only we ourselves.
We must found our own church."[55] Prewar Europe had already seen a most remarkable effort in this direction when
former army captain, Victor Hueber of Prague, founded an
"Organization of Intelligence," of which many well-known
scholars, writers, and artists became nominal members.

But, even if Heinrich Mann agreed with French author
Drieu La Rochelle that it was high time "to establish a new
church, to return to philosophy, to knowledge, to wisdom,"
to the "rule of an academy, wisdom as power,"[56] and thereby also to the "Dictatorship of Reason," he did not by any
means demand a new political, religious, or professional organization. The "infallible faith," the "unity of idea," and
the joyous "mission," which was to emanate from the church
of literature, referred simply to the fruits of faith in the
literary tradition. The prewar public, although often brushed
off by its artists in the course of maintaining their literary
aloofness, owed its moral solidarity as a bourgeoisie to the
remnants of this faithful trust. In the Germany of 1923,

there was no such public that might have heard the call of the "spirit." Since literary tradition had been destroyed along with the bourgeoisie as a historically conscious carrier of educational institutions, the task of passing on the "true faith" fell in fact to a tiny group of prophets. One of them was Heinrich Mann. The heritage of his political period was limited for him to the knowledge of a legend that had called him to be the prophet of the collapse of the Old World.

3 Building the Monument (1926-1946)

Eugénie, Es kommt der Tag, Empfang bei der Welt, Der Atem

IN1925 Heinrich Mann commented on "Spiritual and Intellectual Leanings in Germany," saying: "Since the foundation of the Republic, older poets have been invited to official festivities, even if only to serve as melancholy reminders of better days. People even read them from melancholy."[1] When the Prussian Academy of Arts chose him as its first chairman for literature, it had entrusted a rather unseasonable person with this office. While the newly created institution of a "literary presidency" might have fulfilled the very "demand of the political hour," as ironically raised by Thomas Mann in 1918,[2] Heinrich Mann the writer was completely occupied with finding the appropriate words for a world that, for the most part, greeted literature and poetry with skepticism. This skepticism, however, could by no means be compared with the relationship existing between the "wicked" prewar author and his upright public. The writer of the turn of the century—often a man of inherited income, for whom literary and aesthetic pursuits were sort of a hobby—lived, even as a "pariah of the elite," still one of the "last forms of a bourgeois existence."[3] Also the bourgeois ideal of education had provided both writer and public with a common set of values. This standard was accepted even by those wretches who could not even faintly hope ever to meet it and therefore were ridiculed without mercy whenever possible by the literary greats of the day. In the eyes of their public, however, mockers were only fulfilling their assigned function, and the more biting their ridicule, the more certain the proof that they were acting according to the rules of the game.

With the destruction of the old bourgeoisie through the war and the political and economic events of the postwar times, this function ceased to exist, although these events did not strike directly at the literary trade. Despite inflation and economic crisis, the publishing and book-selling business flourished thanks to the revival of pocket book production and the aid of organizations like the book clubs. Also, large segments of the public still showed the bourgeois affections. Yet, the dialogue between the older authors and readers of the twenties took on an increasingly platonic nature. Before 1914, the bourgeoisie had been such a self-evident entity in the German social framework that it tended constantly to become identical with mankind in general. After 1918, the bourgeoisie became either an ideal or an anathema. In any event, it was always understood as something thoroughly alien. Thus, the twenties became the great time for constructing literary myths, and an era of mission and of legend.[4]

Heinrich Mann's bewilderment as a writer is reminiscent of the beginner's uncertain questioning, around 1900, as to which path ought to be taken through the land of modern literature in order to play the role of author according to the demands of the time. But the cause for concern was quite different in these two situations. The distress felt by the young Heinrich Mann was quite simply the reaction of a rather helpless beginner, who measured his own potential achievements against his own earlier reading, saw the future author as developing progressively out of the zealous reader, was entangled in problems of content and form, and had not yet found out how to formulate what he himself had to say as an author. Obviously, the finished writer no longer confronted such technical difficulties. But while everything depended, for the younger writer, on finding out just what he had to say, the developed writer now faced the equally ticklish question of whether what he had to say was still in demand.

This question has not only biographical but also social significance as well. At the beginning of this study, a break in socioliterary tradition was mentioned, with which the generation stepping on the scene around the turn of the century had been obliged to come to terms. This break in socioliterary tradition, however, lay about fifty years in the past, and, in addition, the gap in continuity existed in the case of Heinrich Mann as in that of his young colleagues between their work and that of the older authors. But around 1925 the new break was part of Mann's immediate personal experience, and, moreover, the historical caesura now fell between his own present position as an author and his equally personal position as an author before 1914. Part of his personality as a writer, achieved at great effort, started to slough off. It became an almost physically tangible phenomenon, though he could not casually surrender that portion of his literary self.

If this peculiar process is considered in the light of the author's relationship to his public, then the difference between Mann's situation as a writer around 1900 and his position around 1925 becomes even clearer. The revolution of 1848 had not substantially altered the social layers of the reading public. Socially, the majority of readers had remained the same bourgeoisie for which authors had written before that date. Only its position in public life had changed insofar as the bourgeoisie had manifested its existence politically, albeit with only slight success.

The writer could therefore no longer play the role of a

secret accomplice of his public, but stood unmasked as its
ally as long as he continued to produce "bourgeois literature." That alone would have been sufficient to explain his
flight into the esoteric existence of the "artist." In addition,
just as the gap between his life and his work was closed, the
former spectacular rise into higher social regions became impossible for him. While the relationship between author and
public was only slightly touched by the revolution and the
rise of the bourgeoisie, the relationship of the postrevolution
writers to their prerevolution literary models was decisively
altered. The feeling of a break in socioliterary tradition,
which was prevalent between 1850 and 1900, arose almost
exclusively from the aspect of opportunities for social advancement enjoyed by the prevolution men of letters, whose
passage from "men of genius" to "men of rank" began to
shine with heroic glory as it receded further and further into
history.[5]

From this viewpoint the fear of the young Heinrich Mann
can be well understood that the ill-mannered rage of naturalism around 1890 would prematurely topple the aristocratic
superstructure of bourgeois literature. Equally well comprehensible, however, is the pride with which Thomas Mann, at
the age of fifty in 1926, championed, in an open letter to
Bert Brecht, the achievements of that same naturalism as the
high point of the bourgeois art, against the "smidgen of
tempo, dynamic cinematic technique, and the anti-bourgeois
cannibalism" that the young generation had to offer.[6]

The "friendly skirmish" between Thomas Mann and Bert
Brecht is very impressive insofar as the two men themselves
illuminate the essence of the new break in socioliterary tradition of the twenties. Brecht had called his older colleague a
spiritual relative of the novelist Friedrich Spielhagen. Thomas
Mann believed he had invalidated this point when he stated
that he had never read so much as a line of this author's
work. This argument reveals the viewpoint of the older

generation, limited, as shown above, almost entirely to a consideration of the immediate relationship to literary models. But when Brecht distanced himself with almost provoking nonchalance from both Mann and Spielhagen, he was thinking rather of the changed relationship of the author to the public—which arose out of the historical change in the social structure that had existed prior to the break in socioliterary tradition—than of any direct literary linking between authors. For Brecht, the differences in aesthetic rank, on which the older authors had prided themselves so much, sank into insignificance. As a member of the new generation of authors, he saw these differences as existing against a background of an extinct public that had held certain definite notions about literature and poetry. In addition, he acquired no special self-esteem from comparing his work with the achievements of any great literary models. His reluctance in this regard probably stemmed from the fact that, while the titles on Goethe and Schiller might inspire an aristocratic literature of "liberated sons of the bourgeoisie" (Heinrich Mann), a merely literary aristocracy could scarcely inspire anyone to imitation.

In order to put in a formula the situation of a writer about 1900 as compared with his situation about 1925, after the change in his relationship to his literary models and to the public, it can be said: The situation in the late nineteenth century—mutual suspicion between "artist" and burgher, together with the fascination of authors with the heroic past—led writers of that day to see literature as being primarily a demonstration of achievement for themselves. The situation in the early twentieth century—loss of the old public with its inherited standards of literature, as well as the rejection of the aristocratic tradition—led writers of that time to see literature primarily as a demonstration of achievement in the eyes of the public. In any event, the earlier idea of literature, however, was also a social convention as well, i.e., an expectation of a public already initiated into the ideology

of individualism in regard to its writers. The later idea of
literature was above all an expression of the author's subjective feelings on finding himself in a world that had not only
rejected the cult of personality in general but had a special
aversion for "artistic" transcendence as well.

Also, to understand the particular work of Heinrich Mann
in the time of the Weimar Republic and in exile, once again
the ambiguous nature of the writer's position must be kept in
mind. The concepts of what writers and writings should be
like, held by any era, are doubtless conditioned by the social
stratification of the public. Included in this very stratification, however, is the contemporary literary erudition of that
public and its authors, which is noticeable not only in its
influence on writing technique but also in its effect on the
concept of what a writer should be like in the minds of both
author and public. Yet the public is neither able nor required
by its role to formulate this concept. A short backward
glance at the figure of the "artist" makes this point clear. The
public would never have been able to put his antics into
words without thereby dissipating the air of mystery sur-
rounding that figure.

But even if the public had had a vague feeling that this
figure embodied the only possible role for a contemporary
creative writer, it would still have been able to shift the responsibility for its invention and shaping onto the shoulders
of the author. Again his acceptance of the responsibility provided the only possible justification for his activity. The same
dialectical relationship between author and public held true
for the literature of the twenties as well. Even an author like
Brecht, who was a firm adherent of the collectivist ideology,
found himself subjectively in the solitary role of a creative
writer. If, however, an already successful older author like
Heinrich Mann had suddenly embraced this ideology, he
would easily have come under the suspicion of wanting to
contest his younger colleagues the artistic realm he had once

enjoyed and which even their loudly proclaimed renunciations had not changed. This last statement is based on the premise that the perspective of the historically or sociologically oriented observer differs from both that of authors and that of the public and is independent of the mutual interactions between them. The specific objectivity of the sociological approach to literature and poetry makes it possible, among other things, for the critic to retain a consciousness of his own distance from both author and that author's public, thus to become aware of the double aspect of their mutual interactions and to formulate them in substance.[7]

The sociological double aspect Heinrich Mann's work offered during the Weimar Republic consisted of the author's attempt, prior to his exile, to tailor his writings to fit the literary situation of the younger generation of authors, as well as the position of a successful older author who had a considerable body of work to defend. By 1910 he had already become the idol of young writers, just as he had reached the high point of his development from reader to author with *Die kleine Stadt*. Roughly speaking, his adherents were divided at that time, exactly as in that novel, into an aesthetically oriented group whose chief representatives were Benn and Rilke and a politically oriented group of activists clustered around E. Mühsam, K. Hiller, and L. Rubiner. Both groups, although quite independent of one another, agreed completely in the cultivation of the classic anti-bourgeois mentality and mannerisms, without, however, ever asking themselves just what they might have to say to a world from which the bourgeoisie had vanished. While the prewar avant garde drew its anti-bourgeois feelings from a surplus of bourgeois atmosphere and values, the postwar youth had to utilize the objective absence of a bourgeoisie as a subjective opportunity for a new literary beginning.

Heinrich Mann, in his essays, took note of the intellectual

tools employed by this generation with astonishing per-
spicacity and much empathy: their mythology of the "mass,"
born out of the loss of the "educated classes" and nourished
by the diffuse interest in literary ceremonial that unwilling
idleness and moral bewilderment in the potential individual
reader brings about during times of economic and social de-
pression; their "proletarian" pathos, which no less obtrusive
than the sentimental "refinement" of previous years, sought
to disguise the fact that of all professions that of writer had
been the most sharply degraded, both in material terms and
in terms of its status. The noise and haste with which they
scrambled upward revealed themselves, on closer inspection,
as an attempt to move ahead as rapidly as possible, as nobody
expected lasting gratitude from the world around them. Thus
it was also easy to renounce the "bourgeois romanticism" of
fame. Yet it remained uncertain whether this much cited
problem of the generations was really the cause of changes in
the new literature or simply an invention of that literature.
The freshening of literature with the entry into newly discovered areas of life, such as sports and technology, at first
justly welcomed, soon degenerated into mere topical
escapism.[8]

Still Heinrich Mann could not avoid the ungratifying task
to remain in talk not to lose the ear of his contemporaries
and to safeguard his very existence as a writer. Even if the
"moralistic exercises" of his lectures, speeches, and essays
were accompanied by the "smile of doubt," [9] his novels,
novellas, and sketches of the Weimar period showed, nonetheless, that he was sufficiently impressed by the supposed
wishes and customs of his new public to pursue, as an author,
trends that, even as a reader and observer, he had previously
not found worth noticing. In this regard, it is difficult to do
justice to Mann's enormous achievement in self-education. He
turned out pieces of mundane eroticism as well as crime and
detective stories; tales of capitalist manipulations of the

economy, boxing matches, battles in light planes, ghostly confrontations between the generations; descriptions of modern youth, of the new life in the big cities, of the latest fashions and dances, of mass pleasures, of vacation pastimes, etc. Yet, even a summary of just the important subjects would erroneously give the impression that they represented only an intrusion of purely topical or merely fashionable elements or stylistic variations on older motifs.

It must, however, be realized that all these subjects were not simply lying about ready to be picked up by any writer. On the contrary, Mann's use of this material showed his attempt to give form to the era's concept of literature. Through numerous hardships his stories and novels tried to invent that poetic formula of the *Zeitgeist* corresponding to the perceptions of the essays, which seems "objectively" comprehensible to an observer of today. In this context, the novella *Liliane und Paul* deserves special attention. This work is not a Kafkaesque allegory (as Weisstein suggests), [10] but rather, judging by its content, an extension of the discussion of the problem of the generations. The work owes its demonic fascination solely to the fact that the flames of the holocaust, which destroy "the old ones," were also licking at the origin and person of their own creator. Hence it was probably the constantly emphasized "progressive" traits of Mann's work at this time, and above all such painful attacks on his own ego that led even Werner Bergengruen to abandon his role of reserved observer and to remark bitterly that he could not "rid himself of the impression that the sixty-year-old author, in his fear of being left behind the times, is driving himself on in this hopeless race at ever greater cost to his organs." [11] To be sure, Heinrich Mann was not spared occasional self-denial, as he experienced the changed situation of the author in his own personal existence. Previously, his writing had been, as in the case of many of his important contemporaries, a luxurious activity by a person of private means. Now, however, a good part of his activity was devoted to the production of assigned work, since lectures to an audience of policemen or to the League for Human Rights, poetry readings in the Karstadt department store in Berlin, radio talks, and newspaper articles often brought in more than a novel selling poorly.

Properly speaking, Heinrich Mann did not undertake this struggle for existence of his own accord. In the long run, self-denial would have been, in any case, an acquired way of life for a young writer, who observed with considerable astonishment how literature—as a social institution—and literary erudition—as the goal of a flourishing educational system—were gradually becoming self-evident and universal, although the craft of writing did not find in the process any inspired or excited chorus of devotees. All people, under the literary democracy of the Weimar Republic, possessed the right to read and to write. In Prussia, likewise, the new sytem of teacher training introduced in 1924 had bridged the gap between lower and higher education. [12] But with the final banishment of illiteracy from Germany also vanished the special position of literature and, with it, the myth of the *homo literatus.* Henceforth, authorship meant pitched battle. In contrast to the younger generation of authors, however, Heinrich Mann had more to defend than just his daily affairs. He also had to safeguard the reputation of an impressive corpus of works that represented his personal past of thirty years as a writer with all its events, experiences, and achievements. Among these achievements was, of course, his own impassioned encounter with a heroic past in which writers had still enjoyed real and effective social privileges. It is therefore no surprise to hear Mann interested, like Heine, in culture and politics, praise and encourage primary education, while complaining in the next breath as a creative writer about the steadily increasing disinterest in literature.

While the task of the younger generation of writers was to bring heaven and earth in literature together, Heinrich Mann, as a representative of the older generation of authors, had to ponder the problem of how to bring together literary yore and now. [13] And, how better to bring that unity about than through the assertion of the priority of all things spiritual, of the poet's anticipation of reality? This use of the motif of anticipation was familiar to Mann insofar as the memory of the legend of *Der Untertan* was still fresh. It also seemed like a good idea to make a virtue of necessity by divesting the motif of the oppressiveness of its origin and making it a universally valid principle. In 1895, Mann had subscribed to the statement that "spiritual needs always create the material demands, which materialism wishes to make primary." In 1931, the writer continued this train of thought with the words, "Today's books arc tomorrow's deeds, and a precursor of the race to come already lives in the writer." In 1941 he concluded: "The spiritual seems to me to be primary. It comes first in history." [14] If, aided by this principle, one could prove to the astonished public that the contemporary world had been invented "from head to toe," by Hauptmann, Wedekind, Gorki, or Stendhal, just as the second French empire had been invented by Balzac, [15] then the literary past would be rescued for a public that, in regard to its knowledge of literature, was quite undemanding. Also, in this way, an uncontestable place of honor would be made for the traditional techniques of the drama and the novel. If a small part of the prophetic glory descended upon Mann himself, that was entirely permissible since Heinrich Mann's earlier work was likewise a part of the literary past and, as such, had as much right to be preserved as any other. Finally, making oneself a part of the literary tradition was at that time nothing more than a wise limitation of oneself to what was attainable, and the price, in any event, was certainly high enough. In order to obtain his literary immortality, Mann, as already with *Der Untertan,* again took the risk of a "creative betrayal" (Robert Escarpit) of his own work. He put himself

in danger of sacrificing to a short-lived legend the essence of
the work he wished to preserve.

In 1928 Mann made his most charming and determined
attempt to create his own literary tradition with the novel
Eugénie oder Die Bürgerzeit, which stood out above the
other novels of the Weimar period because it subscribed most
strongly to the programmatic principle "Actuality passes, art
remains." [16] This principle in no way contradicted the view
expressed by Mann elsewhere that there was no poetry that
was timeless once it was written. [17] The statement indicated
only a plan or a program, i.e., something that had still to be
implemented in literature. The reconciliation of these apparently contradictory theses in the formula, "Permanence is
equivalent to timeliness in the shape of great art," [18] was
possible since this formula affirmed that any timely literature
would also be active in creating the idea of literature peculiar
to its time—and was thus contributing to that permanence
lying so close to Mann's heart.

The artistic unity enclosing all the aspects of the relationship between writer and public in Mann's present situation, as
sketched above, was technically achieved in this book
through the ambiguity of the title. Eugénie was the name of
the novel's heroine and also that of the historical charade
acted out around Eugénie de Montijo, the wife of Napoleon
III. Finally, this name also recalled Eugénie Mirat, the mistress of Heinrich Heine, for the poet of the play depicted in
the novel bore the significant name von Heines. The switch
from the depicting art work to one depicted by it reminds
rather vaguely of similar techniques employed in *Die kleine
Stadt.* But in *Eugénie* there was no gap between art and life,
between the aesthetic value and the social function of literature. When Heinrich Mann was still living in the bourgeois
era, he saw in the public, at best, ignorant folk with little
understanding for literature. When he wrote of this time sub-
sequently, his idealization of that public went so far as to

present an audience composed of a thoroughly literate bourgeoisie, almost every one of whose members, in contrast to the simple folk of *Die kleine Stadt,* would have been able to take a role in the play depicted or, with a little patience and talent, even to write the play himself.

As a consequence a literature that naively aimed only at entertainment and which was dependent upon a literary language, a code of behavior, and an aesthetic standard, all shared by both author and public, showed to be of little objective value. In *Eugénie* the power of the word was absolute. A drama had the same direct effect on the public as the latest news from the stock exchange, which somewhat compensated dramatic literature for its inability to go much beyond the rank of living pictures. To be sure, the glorifying fiction of the art work depicted corresponded in all its parts neither to the actual literary and historical situation of 1873, the year in which the novel was set, nor, naturally enough, to the situation of 1928, the year of its publication. In its nostalgic reminiscence of the "good old days," the novel passed over in silence the former ambition of authors to show themselves intellectually superior to their public in every possible way, whether through their own brilliance or through ridicule of the public's intellectual limitations. Even Heinrich Mann's first and still awkward novel, *In einer Familie* (1895), had provided circumspect demonstration of the transcendence of literature in that the writer delineated the fiction of a reader "led astray." This shows that the relationship between literature and public toward the end of the previous century was certainly not marked by that golden simplicity that *Eugénie* praised so highly. Despite this praise, however, the novel could not disguise the fact that the intimate relation between a sophisticated writer and an equally sophisticated public remained, for the present, an illusory pipe dream. Heinrich Mann and the public of 1928 simply did not share the same literary and historical baggage.

Part of the stock of "good old days gone by" was the figure of the creative writer, whom Heinrich Mann delineated in *Eugénie*. He was a purely idealistic figure insofar as the local public "saluted its own fame" in the person of an author of dramatic and lyrical trivia; for "what put their souls at his disposal was deep within them like a faith—the belief of many races in their poets." [19] It was part of this poet's tragedy that he who "was full of zeal and good intentions for upholding the bourgeoisie" once had to bring a group of amused merchants to embarrassed silence when he appeared in the role of bearer of ill tidings. But since no one can be the victim of tragedy without possessing some hidden greatness, von Heines' work was not permitted simply to slip away from him and be turned unintentionally against him. It did not suffice merely to point out that this patriotic singer of the victorious Germany of the seventies had spread that faith, without which the enemy's armies "had to tread the path of misery"—as long as his drama could later be subtly transformed into the anticipation of dark days ahead for the German bourgeoisie. On the contrary, it was necessary to give him, from the start, the unerring faith that the subtitle of his work, "Ein *deutsches* Spiel" (italics mine), had been rightly chosen. Von Heines had to be a prophet, one who "saw and pieced together what, for others, remained without meaning." The sight of his burghers had to awaken in him the feeling that, for those who could read the signs correctly, these ordinary men, despite their happy innocence, were already in danger. Respectively, those burghers, who were already indulging in all sorts of dark speculations under the guidance of a demonic charlatan, had to be discomfited when they saw themselves "exposed" by him in almost casual fashion. [20]

Eugénie symbolically depicted the end of the German bourgeoisie, about 1914, through the bankruptcy of the burgher West in 1873. To this purpose, a fictitious writer by the name of von Heines had to anticipate that bankruptcy in a fictitious play, which, as the reader of the novel was given to understand, meant that a real writer, by the name of Heinrich Mann, had creatively anticipated in his work the end of the bourgeois era in Germany. This announcement linked *Eugénie* directly to the legend of *Der Untertan,* without, however, including any of the previously customary references to a possible historical responsibility of the bourgeoisie for its own downfall. In addition, Heinrich Mann was modest enough to give the historical dialectic underlying the play a purely private significance. In *Eugénie* the writer was far more successful in his role as prophet than in his earlier commentary on *Der Untertan,* i.e., the essay on Zola, which had obviously served as a model for his latest book. But when the fictitious poet von Heines sang in such vivid fashion of the decline of the "ancient enemy," and only in a metaphorical aside, i.e., by way of an unsuccessful compliment to the leading character in the title of his play, made it known that all was not well with the German bourgeoisie either, Heinrich Mann was thereby admitting quietly to himself and to his readers that he did not actually believe in a real historical prophecy on the part of the fictitious poet von Heines. The historical prognosis of von Heines was based, practically speaking, on the historical experiences of his creator, and served no other purpose beyond that of mastering and justifying these experiences by means of a subjective logic.

Generally speaking, Heinrich Mann's latest work attempted to plaster over the social and literary break of 1914. The appeal to the conscience of the German bourgeoisie in *Der Untertan* had climaxed in the warning that ill-advised members of this species could be swept into the gutter by the deluge. *Eugénie* was riding on the coattails of this warning when it later ascribed to this calamity the solemn function of a necessary expiation, a view which had already been professed to by *Der Kopf.* Here a turning against history became clearly visible. History, which had once turned the moral preachments in the first volume of *Die Kaiserreich-Trilogie* into political snares, had to be outwitted by drawing a useful moral from a political event. In addition, this moral had to be one which had already been anticipated in Mann's earlier novel. Unfortunately, this assertion was completely groundless.

By setting the action of the novel in a ceremonial past, the author indicated that, in his opinion, the era of the bourgeoisie was forever past. Since historical events had also destroyed these well-meaning representatives of the bourgeoisie, the author could no longer shame anyone with his moral examples and could find no one but himself to recognize the accuracy of his prognosis. The public of the twenties had not always experienced the war as the crushing downfall of the seventy-year dominion of "civic ideals," as had Heinrich Mann,[21] and placed no special value on the successful rescue of bourgeois moral principles into a nonbourgeois world. Rather, this public was inclined to play yet another political joke on Heinrich Mann by seeing, in his justification of the miseries of the war, a defense of the peace terms of the Versailles treaty, and by giving the novel a cool reception for just this reason, as a French magazine attentively noted.[22] To be sure, the deafness of Mann's readers to the lesson that the author thought he was able to draw from the disaster, and their blindness to the author's prophetic calling, which was so brilliantly demonstrated when the calamity arrived as forecast, did not have to prevent them from discovering their potential ideal of writing in the narrative grace and refinement of the book. But perhaps it was just the dislike for aesthetic values—a dislike which was now often being cultivated also by younger authors—that led Heinrich Mann to sum up his personal profit from the novel with the preemptive statement that he would sooner have become a monk than be obliged once again to lead the life of a burgher in world that had suddenly become completely uncivilized.[23]

With this confession, he was attempting to put into words the feeling of being personally exposed to history and his direct reflections thereupon that the bourgeois life, once so familiar as to seem part of the order of nature, had really been something artificial, something created by men and therefore perishable. In his description of Napoleon's activities after his ultimate banishment, he had depicted the only role left to the creative writer in a similar situation.

> Even on St. Helena, he was concerned, above all, about his legend. This concern is something especially bourgeois, for it is something handed down, and which lacks naiveté. In addition to, and outside of the realm of practicality, which does not seem sufficiently presentable, a historical alibi, a special place in the high plan of world history is being looked for. This pursuit is bourgeois, it is "literature."[24]

In view of Heinrich Mann's constant resort to the symbols of cloister and church, a growing estrangement between him and the public can already be noted for the Weimar period, a latent "inner emigration," which was only made explicit by his forced exile in 1933. To be sure, the image of the writer class as a church of the bourgeoisie and of literature as a secular reliquary had pursued Mann the writer from the very beginning of his career. Yet, when Wellkamp of *In einer Familie* read Renan's *Prêtre de Némi,* and Köpf of *Im Schlaraffenland* read the Church Fathers, this represented, from one point of view, only a sort of symbolic hint at the origins of European literature and, from another, at the voluntary and conscious exclusion of the bourgeois public from the supposedly higher rituals of art. In the mid-twenties, Heinrich Mann certainly was still entitled to that symbolic resort to the origins of literature. He actually made use of this claim when he explained, in his lecture on "The Future of Culture," that some "secular monks" would rescue the cultural tradition during the "new kind of Middle Ages which seems to be dawning upon us."[25] His relationship to the public, however, was scarcely still under his arbitrary control. At that time, he found himself rather in danger of being excluded against his will, and his assertion that "the Free Masonry of intellectuals will always spring up once more, wherever the masses have been lured to the wrong side,"[26] only made a virtue of this distress.

After his flight from Germany, Heinrich Mann's admission of inner emigration became, of necessity, even clearer in his *Deutsches Lesebuch,* written in Paris and published in Zurich in 1936 under the portentous title, *Es kommt der Tag.* Although faint hopes for an internal change in Germany still existed until the outbreak of war in 1939, the book did not seem to place too much faith in its title. On the contrary, its author, after his books had been burned and their printing and sale forbidden in Germany, felt more like the apostle Paul confronted by the faltering Corinthians. For, after having quoted a passage from his Epistle, altered to fit the times, Mann complained unreservedly of his own spiritual solitude, which was almost as great as it had been in the Germany he had left behind.

> Out here the spiritual environment has at least something in common with the sojourner. But he does not know his readers, who are scattered over the whole earth. He must appear in strange languages, and he must do without the signs of goodwill and gratitude which he had been accustomed to receive from his public.

Approval by the literary and political representatives of foreign lands was "not like receiving as formerly from people, who had nothing more to offer, the demand for an autograph or sometimes just a tear. Elsewhere one had been somehow united even with stupidity."[27]

Since it was a state that had driven him from his homeland, Heinrich Mann came to agree with Nietzsche that a

church was, under any circumstances, a more reputable institution than the state. [28] Only from such a church did he
expect any sort of salvation for the future. Hence when urg-
ing that Christians cooperate with Socialists, that intellectuals
work together with the "proletariat," and that the literary
clergy should make common cause with the "poor in spirit"
against the bourgeoisie, which he had once praised so highly,
he was less setting forth a political program than just describing a literary pipe dream, since he saw the chief virtue of the
Socialists in their potential for taking over the "older inven-
tory of literature." [29] As any living literature required that an
author and his public share certain definite concepts and fulfill certain clear obligations, and "even understand mere allusions," and as, on the other hand, contemporary literature was unburdening itself of all those writers "who
belong to the breed and school of past writers," it was absolutely necessary to educate "officers for the Socialist revolution" in "underground schools affiliated to the Christian
catacombs." [30]

Conceived on the eve of another war waged on an industrial scale, and immediately prior to the pact between the
German and Russian dictatorships, this utopian idea of a
future "people's state," born out of the spirit of the French
Popular Front of 1936, may seem touchingly naive to readers
of today. Yet it would be an act of unpardonable historical
arrogance to conclude, on looking backwards at the apparently immanent consequence of historical events, that contemporaries of that time have always been surprised or overwhelmed by such events. This explanation would only apply
to Heinrich Mann's anxious efforts, during the First World
War, to bring his legend under subsequent personal control
and thus to put history subjectively at his disposal. But long
before the coming of the Second World War, Mann had awakened to the fact that any literary endeavor is a venture into
history. The situation of Europe in 1936 was already pre-
carious enough to imperil the success of this venture, even

without taking into account the events that were to follow.

While authors of the nineteenth century, out of disgust with their bourgeois public, had insisted simultaneously on the decline of culture and on their own personal vindication before the court of appeal of generations yet to come, Heinrich Mann discovered, after 1933, what it really meant to have all persons needed for the literary life of a country systematically scattered and destroyed. His attempt to spend his monkish solitude producing texts for the "German schoolbooks of the twenty-first century" might seem no less absurd than the efforts of Baudelaire or Nietzsche to escape their own historical situation. Mann's attempt, however, was no longer motivated by personal vanity but sprang from a deeply felt need, as the loss of the public toward which he had usually oriented himself had now been followed by a direct attack on the entire "republic of letters." As far as the "socialist" literature of the future was concerned, "no one knows what it will look like,"[31] so that it could not be taken either for a measure or an unconditional guarantee of permanence. Separated in time from the literary past and the literary future of Germany, and separated in space from its literary present, Mann truly was a "monk" whose only basis for all writ was his own work, which as a historical proof of his own personal existence formed the only secure bridge over the abyss of history.

The first book his brother began after moving to California, the novel *Empfang bei der Welt,* Thomas Mann described as a "spirited social satire, located everywhere and nowhere."[32] Yet the external location of the action was not everywhere or nowhere, but rather a land in which the highways traveled "between tracts of woods, unfinished settlements, the flowering groves of daringly styled mansions, and brief hints of desert"; a land where automobile accidents were already a "weekend exercise" in 1941 and where people were just then singing about the "long way to Tipperary"; a land full of canned goods, ice cream, steaks, chicken, tomato sauce, and baseball players; a land with a nationalized armaments industry and a radio industry financed by advertising. In short, the location was the California of 1941.[33] Yet Thomas Mann's description of the book was entirely correct. The spiritual location of the novel could hardly be America since its author, although living on American soil, received only "insignificant" impressions from that country, was collecting royalties from Soviet Russia, and, in general, believed that the name of a "National Socialist," which had been "usurped" by the contemporary political leaders of Germany, really belonged properly to himself.[34]

For the uninitiated reader, it is certainly no pleasure to battle his way through the thicket of ellipses and apodigmata and the forest of passages in foreign languages and strange asides found in *Empfang bei der Welt.* These features are even more prominent with its successor, *Der Atem,* Heinrich Mann's last completed novel, which for the first time also employed the technique of interior monologue markedly and frequently. The immense literary coding of the text was not, however, a frivolous device employed for its own sake but rather an objective and subjective necessity. The confused political and social situation during and shortly after the war, the author's long absence from his homeland, and his feeling, already noticeable during the Weimar period, of being more and more out of touch with the times, all contributed to his realization that the world of literature could no longer be divided up and portioned out according to simple and clear principles. Yet, if his ambition drove Mann to the attempt to demonstrate the depth of his political and literary erudition—as, for instance, in his fanciful pronouncements on the theme "capitalism and existential philosophy," in which the economic system was viewed not as the cause but rather as the result or the embodiment of a philosophy[35]—then it was indeed advisable to shape the style of both novels from the very start to suit a public of Heinrich Mann devotees. Both books could make no other claim than to be some kind of bottled mail for a possible posterity or a sign of life given to a company of initiates who already had an understanding of Mann's earlier writings and were interested in what might yet appear. Accordingly, the aphoristic commentary on history contained in *Empfang bei der Welt* and *Der Atem* was, ironically dedicated to a select few. "The well-known select few. Whoever does not belong to them knows it from today on," as Mann wrote, and, again, "Not to be forgotten. . . . The allusions are meant for experts."[36]

In his two late works Heinrich Mann can be observed building his own monument. Settings and characters in *Empfang bei der Welt* and *Der Atem* were arranged according to the models of earlier novels, novellas, and dramas. Titles and characters of earlier works were cited, and so many allusions were used that this led to a veritable system of concordances between the old and new testaments of the author. In *Empfang bei der Welt,* Heinrich Mann depicted his relationship with literary posterity through the relationship between an Olympian privy councilor, who bore the name of one of the three kings of the East (as seen from California this description suggested Europe), who came "off the bookshelf," and who was honored by people knowing him from "old pulp novels,"[37] as well as a pair of young lovers firmly convinced that "from no one or from him comes word of our fate." Between grandfather and grandchildren, however, stood the generation of the parents, whose catastrophic activism expressed itself in pronouncements such as "Wherever I am, there can be no failure," or "The struggle of life is its own reward,"[38] and who, in the opinion of the author, apparently had been responsible for the disasters of 1914, 1933, and 1939. Fortunately, the legendary old man was able to leave the young people not only his moral code, in which skepticism and prophecies were mixed as well as ever, but also an inheritance of seven wine casks filled with a million gold pieces each—a respectable little sum even at times when the dollar itself was beginning to soften.

Personally speaking, Heinrich Mann had considerably less to pass on than his Olympian ambassador. He left behind only the testament of a great literary past from which he felt posterity was cut off by a veritable abyss. In 1941 he wrote in *Empfang bei der Welt:* "Even confessions like these do not cancel the strangeness of another existence and cannot undo the seventy years that lie in between."[39] Whatever might have been the disposition of the potential public that Mann would meet on his return to Germany, a new literary beginning with this public would have been impossible for him. Although his name might still have been known to that public, his readers would probably have missed all topical links between that name and the work he had done in the meantime.

Thus, both the first and probably also the last of Mann's books written for this public, despite the aid of technical *tours de force* such as allusions to his earlier works and an inner monologue completely immersed in memories, could do no more than first of all provide a mechanical and latent literary tradition, which might perhaps someday in the minds of receptive readers become once again an organic and manifest link to the past. However limited and laborious the service of Mann's late works to the literary past may have been, this effort did offer the writer every possible freedom in the self-interpretation of his work, as the postwar public would have only hazy ideas of him and his previous productions. It was obvious, therefore, that the picture of his life's work, which came into existence this way, would contain more elements of novelistic fiction than of historical truth; or, to put it less harshly, that the creator of this image tried to bring it into harmony with his latest historical and social experiences.

It was here that Heinrich Mann encountered the other problem of his situation as a writer at that time. The hope of somehow gaining the ear of the postwar public could not conceal from him the fact that a gulf was gradually opening between his own personal convictions at the time and those which he had held in the past. The access to the "religion" of his youth, which, as it has been shown in the beginning, he planned to retain, became increasingly more difficult to accomplish each day. The innumerable "moral deviations" of these "corrupted times" had shaken his moralistic foundations. But without the firm belief in unchanging moral laws, even the game played with aesthetic and amoral villainies lost its meaning. Hence, the former libertine in *Empfang bei der Welt* asked himself broodingly if it was still worthwhile to give away his soul for a "completely rotten society, for persons who show us how shamelessly man exposes himself."[40] The same author who, in his memoirs, thanked Nietzsche for his *Genealogy of Morals,* [41] almost simultaneously tried in *Der Atem* to come to terms with the contemporary reality of the *Will to Power.* For this reason, he chose the old fable of the *rusticus imperans*—the peasant who dreams of being chosen king—and staged it under the title *Il Marchese del Grillo* in a Roman theater at the turn of the century, with the entire action taking place in the dreamy reverie of the heroine of the novel, so that Calderon's drama *Life is a Dream* seemed to be doubly fulfilled here.[42]

But the romantic technique only thinly disguised the seriousness of the situation as Mann perceived it. In contrast to Thomas Mann's novella *Mario und der Zauberer* (1938), no one from the public of this play, conceived after the catastrophe, was able to resist the seduction. Children and people, with their "nimble imagination" but without the inclination to "analyze the pleasures received," ran through the world of this beautiful pipe dream without realizing that they had been deceived just as much as the fool on the stage who was permitted to play the "Herrenmensch" for a single night.[43] To be sure, the educated middle class—represented by the heroine of the novel and her young lover, who jovially ordered a supper for the players from the nearest tavern— seemed to have equally little understanding of the consequences of the odd artistic exercise on the stage. The reader, however, comprehends the brutal meaning of the seemingly pleasant and graceful play as soon as he recalls a statement made in *Empfang bei der Welt* that sounded like a commentary on the doings of the villainous marchese on the stage as well as on the behavior of the audience in the pit: "The cunning elite will always lead, but between this elite and the collective incompetence of the background, the calloused middle classes just watch and let things happen. That is the house."[44]

This statement is remarkable because it tells about how Heinrich Mann believed guilt had to be distributed. In contrast to his brother's view, Heinrich Mann shifted the responsibility from those "Herrenmenschen," risen almost against their will from the masses, onto the shoulders of those influential "men behind the scenes," embodied in *Der Atem* by the court of the marchese. At the same time, the familiar note of self-criticism and apology, significant of Mann's late work, becomes audible once more in his allusion to the bourgeoisie's support of "arts" allegedly contributing to its own ruin. For just as his old thesis of the priority of spiritual acts compelled the writer to conceive of the capitalistic system as an applied philosophy of existence, the same thesis also made him sense the influence of Nietzsche's person and work behind the social manifestations symbolized in the *Marchese del Grillo.* In doing so, however, he touched upon a significant point in his own irrevocable literary past, which only an emphatically critical treatment could save for the future.

The gap between past and present separated Mann from certain political and moral concepts dear to his heart. The same gap, however, also allowed him to recognize how greatly the position of literature and poetry had changed in the age of total war and compulsive buying craze; in the age of the atomic bomb, the film, and the radio. *Empfang bei der Welt* was crowned by the appearance of the "Orchestra of Immortals": Bach, Mozart, Berlioz, Chopin, Verdi, Wagner, Brahms, Tchaikovsky, and Debussy, as masked members of an ensemble, financed by the record industry, whose "atonal processional march" was received with courteously concealed yawns by the crowd at a Beverly Hills party.[45]

Considering the expositions of the first chapters of this study, this scene, in Mann's case, is suitably translated from musical (or "artistic") to literary terms. This shows that his satirical fiction was meant to demonstrate the continuous presence of all painstakingly developed historical styles in modern art. The immortal members of this orchestra, as Mann's argument ran, had paid for their fame with the total lack of any social or historical obligation caused by an inflationary cultural buying craze. To this direful situation, Mann compared an idealized picture of the reception of art in times gone by, when he had one of the main characters of his novel explain that Italy had something even greater than its fame as the nation of *bel canto:* "The unknown masterworks, I mean. Familiar to every child of Italy, they have never crossed its borders."[46] The word "unknown," as the next sentence shows, refers to the non-Italian outside world.

This picture must be called idealized because it actually corresponded only in part to the situation in which Heinrich Mann had found himself as a writer for the greatest part of his life. At the very moment when literature began to reflect the problems of a time that was more or less postliterary, Heinrich Mann invoked the ideals of aesthetic reception in a preliterary world, without making clear to himself or to his readers just why these ideals held so much attraction for him—the reason being, of course, the special status which literature as a newly discovered, supraregional means of communication and tradition was to acquire in a "primeval" world.

It may be sufficient to point out that the entire mystique of the aestheticism of the late nineteenth century had depended for its life on the unwavering assumption that this situation still existed. In the years after World War II, literature began to suffer a basic loss of this special social status, which, in any event, as the citation above admits, had always found its limits in the national or local language. The age of the poet and of the artist ended provisionally with the weekly newsreel and polyglot hit tunes. Perhaps it was this knowledge, more disturbing for the author than for the public, that caused Heinrich Mann to sum up his last novel:

> It was quiet. The brightness of the garden had been blotted. The world slept, numb as in nights of disaster befalling it, when we likewise are tired and lay down the word.[47]

Important Dates in the Life of Heinrich Mann

1871   March 27: born in Lübeck Luiz Heinrich Mann, eldest son of the merchant Thomas Heinrich Mann and his wife Julia, née da Silva-Bruhns.

1884   Trip to St. Petersburg with his uncle.

1889   Completes the *Gymnasium* and obtains his *Abitur*. Training as a book seller in Dresden.

1890   Active for S. Fischer Verlag, Berlin. Occasional studies at the University of Berlin. Undecided between painting and writing.

1891   October 13: death of his father. Family moved to Munich shortly afterwards.

1893   First trip to France. Lengthy stay in Italy, interrupted by frequent visits to sanitaria in Lausanne, Brunnthal in Bavaria, Riva on Lake Garda, brought on by his poor health. Published a literary-political magazine for a short time.

1900   Return to Germany. Active as an author for Albert Langen Verlag, Munich.

1902   Start of his long friendship with Frank Wedekind.

1907   Publisher Paul Cassirer becomes his patron.

1909   Receives assistance from publisher Anton Kippenberg (Insel-Verlag). Sojourn in Nice.

1910   Death of his sister, Carla (born 1881), to whom he had been very close, and who had become an actress.

1914   August 12: marries Czech actress Maria Kanova.

1916   Birth of their daughter, Henriette Marie Leonie.

1917   Active as an author for Kurt Wolff Verlag.

1918   Supports the revolutionary regime of Kurt Eisner in Munich.

Signs the declaration of the "Council of Intellectual Workers."
1923   Participates in the "Entretiens de Pontigny." Meeting with André Gide and Felix Bertaux. Speaks at the Constitution Celebration in Dresden.
1924   Interview with President Masaryk in Prague .
1925   Moves to Berlin. Active as an author for Paul Zsolnay Verlag. First trip to the Pyrenees.
1927   Speaks before the League for Human Rights and at the Congress of Radical Socialist Parties in Paris; journeys from there to the Pyrenees once more.
1931   President of the literary division of the Prussian Academy of Arts. Second marriage to Nelly Kröger. Interview with Foreign Minister Briand in Paris.
1932   Nominated by Kurt Hiller for the office of *Reichspräsident* in Carl von Ossietzky's *Weltbühne*. His refusal and open support of Hindenburg bring him the reproaches of the literary and political Left.
1933   February 15: expulsion from the Academy. February 20: flight to France, taking up residence chiefly in Nice. Works on staff of *Dépêche de Toulouse* until 1936 and helps to establish the French Front Populaire as well as the German Popular Front Movement in Exile. His chief work at the time (the novel of King Henry IV) is published in Amsterdam by Querido.
1940   Flight over the Pyrenees to Lisbon. Embarks for America with his wife. Arrives in New York City on October 13. Settles in Los Angeles.
1945   In the following years he is given an honorary doctorate in absentia by the Humboldt University in East Berlin. Winner of the East German State Prize, first class, and president of the East Berlin Academy of Arts.
1950   March 12: dies in Santa Monica, California, shortly before his planned return to Germany. His works are now published in East Berlin by Aufbau Verlag and in Hamburg by Claassen Verlag.

The Writings of
Heinrich Mann

1. Novels:

1a. *In einer Familie.* Munich, 1894.
 b. *In einer Familie.* Berlin, 1894.
 c. *In einer Familie.* Authorized new edition with a preface by the author. Berlin, 1924.
2a. *Im Schlaraffenland. Ein Roman unter feinen Leuten.* Munich 1900-1901.
 b. *Im Schlaraffenland. Ein Roman unter feinen Leuten.* Unabridged new edition with a preface by the author and an introduction by the publisher, L. Dunin. Berlin, 1929.
3a. *Die Göttinnen oder die drei Romane der Herzogin von Assy.* Munich, 1902-1903.
 b. *Die Göttinnen oder die drei Romane der Herzogin von Assy.* With concluding remarks by A. Kantorowicz. Berlin, 1957.
 c. *Die Göttinnen oder die drei Romane der Herzogin von Assy.* Hamburg, 1957.
4a. *Die Jagd nach Liebe.* Munich, 1903.
 b. *Die Jagd nach Liebe.* Berlin, 1957.
 c. *Die Jagd nach Liebe.* With concluding remarks by A. Kantorowicz. Hamburg, 1957.
5a. *Professor Unrat oder das Ende eines Tyrannen.* Munich, 1905-1906.
 b. *Professor Unrat oder das Ende eines Tyrannen.* Berlin, 1930.

   c. *Professor Unrat oder das Ende eines Tyrannen.* Authorized new edition with a preface by W. Kiewert. Berlin & Stuttgart, 1947.

   d. *Professor Unrat oder das Ende eines Tyrannen.* Hamburg, 1951.

  6. *Zwischen den Rassen.* Berlin, 1907.

  7. *Die kleine Stadt.* Leipzig, 1909.

  8. *Die Armen.* Leipzig & Munich, 1917.

 9a. *Der Untertan.* Leipzig & Munich, 1918.

  b. *Der Untertan.* Unabridged new edition, with a preface by the author and an introduction by the publisher, L. Dunin, Berlin, 1929.

10. *Der Kopf.* Vienna & Berlin, 1925.

11. *Eugénie oder die Bürgerzeit.* Vienna & Berlin, 1928.

12a. *Mutter Marie.* Vienna & Berlin, 1930.

  b. *Mutter Marie.* With a preface by L. Dunin. Berlin, 1932.

13. *Die grosse Sache.* Potsdam, 1930.

14. *Ein ernstes Leben.* Vienna & Berlin, 1932.

15. *Die Jugend des Königs Henri Quatre.* Amsterdam, 1935.

16. *Die Vollendung des Königs Henri Quatre.* Amsterdam, 1938.

17. *Lidice.* Mexico City, 1943.

18a. *Der Atem.* Amsterdam, 1949.

  b. *Der Atem.* Hamburg, 1962.

19a. *Empfang bei der Welt.* Berlin, 1956.

  b. *Empfang bei der Welt.* Hamburg, 1962.

20a. *Die traurige Geschichte von Friedrich dem Grossen* (posthumous novel in dialogue form). Published by the Deutsche Akademie der Künste in honor of the tenth anniversary of Heinrich Mann's death, with a preface by B. Uhse. Berlin, 1960.

  b. *Die traurige Geschichte von Friedrich dem Grossen.* Hamburg, 1962.

2. Novellas:

21. *Das Wunderbare.* Munich, 1897.

22. *Ein Verbrechen.* Leipzig, 1898.

23. *Flöten und Dolche.* Munich, 1905.

24. *Mnais und Ginevra.* Munich, 1906.

25. *Schauspielerin.* Vienna, 1906.
26. *Stürmische Morgen.* Munich, 1906.
27. *Die Bösen.* Leipzig, 1908.
28. *Das Herz.* Leipzig, 1911.
29. *Die Rückkehr vom Hades,* Leipzig, 1911.
30. *Auferstehung.* Leipzig, 1913.
31. *Bunte Gesellschaft.* Munich, 1917.
32. *Der Vater.* In *Der neue Roman. Ein Almanach.* Leipzig & Munich, 1917.
33. *Der Sohn.* Hanover, 1919 (identical with no. 32).
34a. *Die Ehrgeizige.* In *Forum,* no. 7. Munich, 1914-1915.
   b. *Die Ehrgeizige.* Book edition. Munich, 1920.
35. *Die Tote.* Pullach near Munich, 1920.
36. *Abrechnungen.* Berlin, 1924.
37. *Der Jüngling.* Vienna & Berlin, 1924.
38a. *Kobes.* In *Neue Rundschau* I. Berlin, 1925.
   b. *Kobes.* Book edition. Berlin, 1925.
39. *Liliane und Paul.* Vienna & Berlin, 1926.
40. *Sie sind jung.* Vienna & Berlin, 1929.
41. *Der Tyrann. Die Branzilla.* With concluding remarks by F. Salten. Leipzig, 1929.
42. *Suturp.* Berlin, 1929.
43. *Der Freund.* Vienna, 1931.
44. *Die Welt der Herzen.* Potsdam, 1932.
45. *Eine Liebesgeschichte.* Published by K. Lemke (on behalf of the Heinrich Mann Gesellschaft für zeitgenössische Dichtung). Munich, 1953.
46. *Das gestohlene Dokument.* Berlin, 1957.

3. Selected Essays and Similar Works:

47. "Bourget als Kosmopolit." *Gegenwart,* vols. 45-46. Berlin, 1894.
48. "Alphonse Daudet über das Theater." *Gegenwart,* vols. 45-46. Berlin, 1894.
49. "Barbey d'Aurevilly." *Gegenwart,* vols. 47-48. Berlin, 1895.
50. "Beiträge." As editor of the magazine *Das Zwanzigste Jahrhundert,* vols. V, VI. Berlin & Zurich, 1894-1895 and 1895-1896. In first and second numbers of each.

51. "Kleine Selbstbiographie." *Verlagskatalog* of A. Langen. Munich, 1904.
52. "Les Liaisons Dangereuses." *Zukunft,* no. 50. Berlin, 1905.
53a. "Eine Freundschaft (G. Flaubert und G. Sand)." *Zukunft,* no. 52. Berlin, 1905.
   b. "Eine Freundschaft (G. Flaubert und G. Sand)." As preface to the German edition of their correspondence. Munich, 1905.
54a. "Flaubert und die Kritik." *Nord und Süd,* no. 1. Berlin, 1908.
   b. "Flaubert und die Kritik." *Aktion.* Berlin, 1916.
   c. "Flaubert und die Kritik." Book edition in *Geist. Beste Essays der Weltliteratur.* Berlin, 1917.
   d. "Flaubert und die Kritik." As preface to *G. Flaubert, Briefwechsel.* Potsdam, 1919.
55a. "Geist und Tat." *Pan (II),* no. 5. Berlin, 1910-1911.
   b. "Geist und Tat." *Das Ziel. Aufruf zu tätigem Geist.* Munich, 1916.
56a. "Der französische Geist (Voltaire-Goethe)." *Freiheit und Arbeit* (art and literature collection published by the Internationales Komitee zur Unterstützung der Arbeitslosen). With a preface by E. Bernstein. Leipzig & Zürich, 1910.
   b. "Der französische Geist (Voltaire-Goethe)." *Aktion.* Berlin, 1912.
57. "Reichstag." *Pan (II),* no. 5. Berlin, 1910-1911.
58. "Flaubert's Monolog." *Forum,* no. 1. Munich & Berlin, 1914-1915.
59. "Zola." *Weisse Blätter,* pp. 1312ff. Leipzig, 1915.
60. "Flaubert und die Herkunft des modernen Romans." *Der neue Roman. Ein Almanach.* Leipzig & Munich, 1917.
61. *Macht und Mensch. Ein politisches Zeitbuch.* Leipzig & Munich, 1919.
62a. "Deutschland und Frankreich-Antwort an J. Rivière." *Neue Rundschau* II. Berlin, 1923.
   b. "Deutschland und Frankreich-Antwort an J. Rivière." *Diktatur der Vernunft.* Berlin, 1923.
63a. "Europa—Reich über den Reichen." *Neue Rundschau* II. Berlin, 1923.
   b. "Europa—Reich über den Reichen." *Diktatur der Vernunft.* Berlin, 1923.
   c. "Europa—Reich über den Reichen." Shortened extract

under the title, "Gierigstenherrschaft." *Geistige Politik.* Leipzig & Vienna, 1924.

64. *Diktatur der Vernunft.* Berlin, 1923.
65. "Anatole France—Skepsis und Liebe." *Münchner Neueste Nachrichten.* October 21, 1924.
66. "Victor Hugo und seine Romane." *Neue Zürcher Zeitung.* December 13, 1925.
67. "Die neuen Gebote." *Literarische Welt,* no. 3. Berlin, 1927.
68. "Die Literatur und die deutsch-französische Verständigung." *Literarische Welt,* no. 14. Berlin, 1927.
69. "Dichtkunst und Politik." *Neue Rundschau,* II. Berlin, 1928.
70. "Politischer Wille und Gestaltung." *Literarische Welt,* no. 16. Berlin, 1929.
71. "Entdeckung Zolas." *Literarische Welt.* no. 39. Berlin, 1929.
72. *Sieben Jahre. Chronik der Gedanken und Vorgänge 1921-1928.* Vienna & Berlin, 1929.
73. "Was ist eigentlich ein Schriftsteller? " *Propyläen.* Munich, 1931.
74. "Ein junger Franco-Europäer: Philippe Soupault." *Literarische Welt,* no. 7-10. Berlin, 1931.
75. "Hermann Kesten." *Literarische Welt,* no. 18. Berlin, 1931.
76. "G. Flaubert—50 Jahre nach seinem Tode." *Literarische Welt,* no. 19. Berlin, 1931.
77. "Käufliche Dämonie." *Literarische Welt,* no. 40-43. Berlin, 1931.
78. *Geist und Tat. Franzosen 1780-1930.* Potsdam, 1931.
79. "Der Schriftsteller und der Staat." *Neue Rundschau* I. Berlin, 1931.
80a. "Das Bekenntnis zum Übernationalen." *Neue Rundschau* II. Berlin, 1932.
   b. "Das Bekenntnis zum Übernationalen." Book edition with other essays. Vienna, 1933.
81. *Der Hass. Deutsche Zeitgeschichte.* Amsterdam. 1933.
82. *Es kommt der Tag. Deutsches Lesebuch.* Zürich, 1936.
83. *Mut.* Paris, 1939.
84. "Die französische Revolution und Deutschland." *Aufbau,* no. 3. Berlin, 1945.

85a. *Ein Zeitalter wird besichtigt.* Stockholm, 1945-1946.
  b. *Ein Zeitalter wird besichtigt.* Frankfurt, 1946.
  c. *Ein Zeitalter wird besichtigt.* Berlin, 1947.
86. "Mein Bruder." *Kulturaufbau,* p. 85. Düsseldorf, 1950.
87. "Literatur und Gesellschaft." *Volksbibliothekar,* p. 131. Berlin & Leipzig, 1950.

4. Collections:

88. *Die Novellen.* 2 vols. Leipzig & Munich, 1916-1917.
89. *Gesammelte Romane und Novellen.* 12 vols. Leipzig & Munich, 1917.
90. *Gesammelte Werke.* 12 vols. Vienna, Berlin & Leipzig, 1925-1932. (Contains: *Im Schlaraffenland, Die Göttinnen, Die Jagd nach Liebe, Professor Unrat, Zwischen den Rassen, Die kleine Stadt, Mutter Marie, Flöten und Dolche, Das Herz, Die Rückkehr vom Hades,* and *Das öffentliche Leben.*)
91. *Das Kaiserreich.* A trilogy in two volumes (1. *Der Untertan* and *Die Armen,* 2. *Der Kopf*). Vienna, 1931.
92a. *Ausgewählte Werke in Einzelausgaben.* 12 vols. With concluding remarks and bibliographic comments by A. Kantorowicz. Berlin, 1951-1956. (Contains: *Im Schlaraffenland, Professor Unrat, Zwischen den Rassen, Die kleine Stadt, Der Untertan, Eugénie, Ein ernstes Leben, Die Jugend des Königs Henri Quatre, Die Vollendung des Königs Henri Quatre,* novellas, plays, and essays.)
  b. *Ausgewählte Werke in Einzelausgaben.* Hamburg, 1958.

Notes

Notes to the Introduction

1. Jean-Paul Sartre, *Was ist Literatur?* (Hamburg, 1958), p. 48.
2. Ibid., p. 92.
3. Ibid., p. 90.
4. Cf. Joseph von Eichendorff, *Ahnung und Gegenwart,* Manesse Ausgabe, pp. 203, 219, and Goethe, *Werke,* Festausgabe (Leipzig, 1926), X:132.
5. Robert Escarpit, *Das Buch und der Leser* (Cologne-Opladen, 1961). pp. 108ff.
6. Ibid., p. 111.
7. Sartre, *Was ist Literatur?*, p. 81.
8. Ibid., p. 45.

Notes to Chapter 1

(The writings of Heinrich Mann will be cited in the notes only by title. The numbers in parentheses that follow refer to the arrangement of the works in the list on p. 121, where complete data are given.)

1. *Ein Zeitalter wird besichtigt* (85c), pp. 174, 180.
2. Schmitt-Fricke, *Deutsche Literaturgeschichte in Tabellen* (Bonn, 1952), vol. III, table 2. See also W. Kayser, "Das literarische Leben der Gegenwart," *Deutsche Literatur in unserer Zeit* (Göttingen, 1959), pp. 9-10.
3. F. Schlawe, *Literarische Zeitschriften 1885-1910* (Stuttgart, 1961), p. 3.

4. Sartre, *Was ist Literatur?*, p. 101.
5. "Beiträge" (50), VI/II:376.
6. "Voltaire-Goethe" (92a), XI:18.
7. Cf. Sartre, *Was ist Literatur?*, pp. 79-83.
8. "Beiträge" (50), VI/I:404.
9. Thomas Mann, *Betrachtungen eines Unpolitischen* (Berlin, 1918), p. 117.
10. "Beiträge" (50), V/I:189.
11. Ibid., VI/I:18.
12. *In einer Familie* (1a), p. 61. Cf. also Heinrich Mann's essay "Reaction! " in "Beiträge" (50), V/II:1ff. and Nietzsche's aphorism about "Die Reaction als Fortschritt" in the edition of his work published by K. Schlechta, Munich, 1956, I:466.
13. *In einer Familie* (1a), pp. 112, 194, 242.
14. "Beiträge" (50), V/II:83-84.
15. Heinrich Mann usually passed over this novel in silence but, in 1924, declared himself ready for a new edition with an apologetic preface so that readers might take his attitude seriously despite the technical shortcomings of the novel.
16. "Beiträge" (50), V/II:4, 8.
17. Ibid., VI/II:107. This is an unsigned reply to K. Bleibtreu, which, judging by its subject matter, can probably be ascribed to Mann.
18. Ibid., V/II:6.
19. Letter of March 3, 1943, to A. Kantorowicz, in H. Jhering, *Heinrich Mann* (Berlin, 1951), p. 142.
20. "Beiträge" (50), V/II:352.
21. *Im Schlaraffenland* (92a), I:94, 117-118, 142ff., 284, 332-333, 335-336, 339-340.
22. Ibid., p. 301.
23. K. Martens, *Literatur in Deutschland* (Berlin, 1910), p. 129, and J. Ettlinger, "Heinrich Manns *Im Schlaraffenland,*" *Litterarisches Echo* (Berlin, 1901), pp. 334-336.
24. *Im Schlaraffenland* (92a), I:60.
25. Essay on Flaubert (92a), XI:91.
26. *Die Jagd nach Liebe* (4a), p. 433.
27. *Im Schlaraffenland* (92a), I:22.
28. W. Ziegenfuss, *J. J. Rousseau* (Erlangen, 1952), pp. 85, 139, and Heinrich Mann's essay on Voltaire and Goethe (92a), XI:18.
29. Recently, Sartre (*Was ist Literatur?*, pp. 79, 83, 90), has taken up this theme in regard to R. Caillois' book *L'homme et le sacré* (Paris, 1950 and 1955). V. Pareto was the first to develop this

idea in his work *Le mythe vertuiste et la littérature immorale* (Paris, 1911).

30. "Beiträge" (50), V/II:92-93. This article is also ascribed to Mann in the bibliography of U. Weisstein, *Heinrich Mann* (Tübingen, 1962). Heinrich Mann felt that this contention was supported by the¹ fact that the *Sozialdemokrat,* on May 9, 1895 (likewise cited in Weisstein, p. 397) had called Hauptmann's drama "the very flesh and spirit of Social Democracy."

31. Ibid., p. 8.

32. Cf. Nietzsche *Werke,* Schlechta ed., I:100. There are also overtones of Paul de Lagarde (*Politische Aufsätze,* 1874, and *Deutsche Schriften,* 1878-1881).

33. Heinrich Heine, *Werke* (Vienna & Leipzig, 1890), VI:42-43.

34. Cf. Sartre, *Was ist Literatur?,* p. 57, in regard to the writings of the seventeenth-century French moralists that deal with the misery of the peasants of their country.

35. Reply to the magazine *Nord und Süd* (Berlin, 1908), no. 4, p. 72.

36. Cf. Weisstein, *Heinrich Mann,* p. 36, n. 66.

37. In his "Beiträge" (50), VI/II:105, Mann linked the superficial pursuit of pleasure, gratified in the theater, to the general shallowness of culture in the city.

38. Letter of March 3, 1943, to A. Kantorowicz, cited in Jhering, *Heinrich Mann,* p. 142.

39. Ibid., pp. 78, 141-142.

40. See Thomas Mann's letter to his brother, December 30, 1909, in A. Kantorowicz, *Heinrich und Thomas Mann* (Berlin, 1956), p. 84.

41. *Wiener Tageszeitung* (Vienna, 1903), no. 122.

42. "Kleine Selbstbiographie" (51), p. 92.

43. *Professor Unrat* (92a), I:437.

44. Cf. H. Sinsheimer, *Heinrich Manns Werk* (Munich, 1921), p. 29.

45. Thomas Mann's letter to his brother, February 18, 1905, in Kantorowicz, *Heinrich und Thomas Mann,* p. 82.

46. Cf. for what follows L. L. Schücking, *Die Soziologie der literarischen Geschmacksbildung* (Leipzig & Berlin, 1931), pp. 28ff.

47. Essay on Flaubert (92a), XI:106.

48. "Kleine Selbstbiographie" (51), p. 92, and *Ein Zeitalter wird besichtigt* (85c), p. 277, where it is also stated that the figure of Dorlenghi symbolizes the creative activity of Puccini.

49. "Beiträge" (50), VI/II:250.

50. *Ein Zeitalter wird besichtigt* (85c), p. 143.

51. This content appears again in the novella with this title ([92a],

VIII:156ff). According to U. Weisstein (*Heinrich Mann,* p. 100), there is a sketch for a corresponding opera libretto in the Heinrich Mann archive in Berlin. In material, *Die kleine Stadt* is most reminiscent of Gottfried Keller's tale, *Romeo und Julia auf dem Dorfe,* or of Richard Wagner's lost early work, *Das Liebesverbot oder die Novize von Palermo.*

52. See the discussion between Heinrich Mann and L. D. Frost, in *Zukunft* (Berlin, 1910), 70:116-119, 265-266.
53. Essay on Flaubert (92a), XI:79.
54. *Die kleine Stadt* (92a), III:209.
55. Ibid., pp. 147, 194.
56. Cf. Ziegenfuss, *J. J. Rousseau,* p. 90.
57. Essay on Flaubert (92a), XI:93.
58. *Zwischen den Rassen* (92a), II:144-145.
59. Thomas Mann's letter to his brother, December 30, 1909, in Kantorowicz, *Heinrich und Thomas Mann,* p. 84. The novella *Die Rückkehr vom Hades,* which appeared in 1911, two years after *Die kleine Stadt,* still mirrors clearly Mann's disappointment in this regard.
60. W. Rath, "Heinrich Manns *Kleine Stadt,*" *Kunstwart* II (Munich, 1910):23ff.
61. *Die kleine Stadt* (92a), III:206.

Notes to Chapter 2

1. *Ein Zeitalter wird besichtigt* (85c), pp. 181, 215. The novella *Gretchen* (92a), IX:195ff., is the prelude to *Der Untertan.*
2. *Die Jagd nach Liebe* (4a), p. 2. Cf. n. 33 to chapter 1.
3. *Im Schlaraffenland* (92a), I:22.
4. *Der Untertan* (92a), IV:6, 12, 80.
5. K. Martens, *Literatur in Deutschland,* p. 115. There is a pun involved in Hessling's definition of the novel as an "un-German" art, the German word for "novel" being "Roman."
6. *Der Untertan* (92a), p. 278. A code of manners was one of Mann's favorite arguments. See *Im Schlaraffenland* (92a), I:95.
7. Ibid., p. 338. There are serious discussions of Wagner and Nietzsche by Mann in these essays (50), V/II:143, VI/I:393, VI/II:245; and in *Ein Zeitalter wird besichtigt* (85c), pp. 162ff.
8. Cf. Schücking, *Die Soziologie der literarischen Geschmacksbildung,* p. 38, and J. Bab, *Befreiungs-Schlacht* (Stuttgart, 1928), pp. 53-54.
9. Pp. 133ff., reprinted in (92a), XII:7ff.

10. *Der Untertan* (92a), IV:230. Here Heinrich Mann was pleading in favor of the imperial family and against Social Democracy. In a later essay, where he commented on *Der Kopf,* Mann expressed the same sentiments. ("Unser gemeinsames Problem" [92a], XII:289.)
11. Weisstein, *Heinrich Mann,* p. 117.
12. See F. Schlawe, *Literarische Zeitschriften 1910-1933* (Stuttgart, 1962), p. 87.
13. Cf. Weisstein, *Heinrich Mann,* p. 115.
14. L. Rubiner, "Heinrich Manns *Untertan," Aktion* (Berlin, 1914), pp. 335ff.
15. See *Zeit im Bild* (Munich, 1914), no. 33, p. 1666, where the designations "conclusion" and "end" are expressly used. (This passage corresponds to [92a], IV:409.)
16. Cf. V. Mann, *Wir waren fünf* (Constance, 1949), p. 364.
17. Cf. the essays, "Geist und Tat" and "Der französische Geist" (92a), XI:9, 18.
18. See, for instance, the passage beginning "And then the Empire fell . . . " (92a), XI:166-167.
19. *Ein Zeitalter wird besichtigt* (85c), p. 181.
20. Weisstein, *Heinrich Mann,* p. 116. In his later speeches, Heinrich Mann expressed his feelings about personal participation in the war ([92a], XII:369). In the novel *Eugénie,* the author had some fictitious veterans of the 1914-1918 war testify as to how right he had been in his interpretation of the omens of that period (92a), V:183.
21. Speech delivered before the League for Human Rights (92a), XII:369.
22. Letter to his brother, January 5, 1918, cited in Kantorowicz, *Heinrich und Thomas Mann,* pp. 37, 40.
23. Essay on Zola (92a), XI:166.
24. See Jhering, *Heinrich Mann,* p. 143.
25. *Die Armen* (8), p. 295.
26. Ibid., pp. 30, 69, 228, 246.
27. F. Diederichs, "Heinrich Manns *Untertan," Die neue Zeit* (Berlin, 1919), pp. 444ff.
28. These criticisms are also found in Jhering (*Heinrich Mann,* pp. 66ff.) and in Weisstein (*Heinrich Mann,* p. 129). The concepts of Social Darwinism, however, are already present in the "Beiträge." The learning of Latin serves only as a symbol for the general process of learning, which always involves coming to terms with traditional values.

29. *Die Armen* (8), pp. 120ff.
30. Diederichs, loc. cit.
31. "Uns gemeinsam erinnern" (92a), XII:294. The response of the "independent" leftists, who had greeted *Der Untertan* with jubilation in the prewar days, was certainly no more favorable. See L. Rubiner, "Heinrich Manns *Die Armen*," *Aktion* (Berlin, 1918), pp. 29ff.
32. Diederichs, loc. cit.
33. *Ein Zeitalter wird besichtigt* (85c), p. 172. Thomas Mann also spoke occasionally of the fear of impending economic ruin. (Letter to his brother, August 7, 1914, cited in Kantorowicz, *Heinrich und Thomas Mann*, pp. 106-107.)
34. *Die Jagd nach Liebe* (4a), p. 530; *Die Göttinnen* (3a), II:330 and III:274.
35. Speech before the League for Human Rights (92a), XII:368.
36. *Der Kopf* (10), pp. 95, 272.
37. "Erinnerungen an Frank Wedekind" (92a), XI:407.
38. "Unser gemeinsames Problem" (92a), XII:289-290.
39. *Der Kopf* (10), pp. 526, 598.
40. Ibid., p. 633.
41. *Geist und Tat* (92a), XI:14.
42. See, for instance, O. Flake, "Heinrich Manns *Der Kopf*," *Neue Rundschau* (Berlin, 1925), pp. 865ff.
43. Martens (*Literatur in Deutschland*, p. 112), for instance, found this classification no hindrance to assuring Mann that he could tell a story "poetically"—a pronouncement that Martens considered the highest praise possible.
44. *Diktatur der Vernunft* (64), p. 19.
45. Ibid., pp. 26-27, 71.
46. Ibid., p. 20.
47. See, for instance, "Essay über Napoleon" (92a), XI:140; "Das Bekenntnis zum Übernationalen" (92a), XII:501; and "Es kommt der Tag" (82), p. 208.
48. *Kaiserreich und Republik* (92a), XII:62.
49. *Diktatur der Vernunft* (64), p. 18. Cf. the novella *Kobes* (92a), IX:310, where the same idea also appeared. It is interesting to note that Mann had nothing to say about the deflation crisis of 1929-1931. He confined himself to criticizing Chancellor Luther for using the Dawes-Young Plan funds to extend credits to industry.
50. *Eugénie* (92a), V:62.

51. *Kaiserreich und Republik* (92a), XII:53.
52. *Der Kopf* (10), p. 593.
53. Ibid., pp. 595-596.
54. See F. Schlawe, *Literarische Zeitschriften 1910-1933* (Stuttgart, 1962), p. 92; and F. Muckermann, "Dichtung und Grossindustrie," *Gral* (Essen, 1924), pp. 265ff.
55. *Diktatur der Vernunft* (64), pp. 47-48.
56. Ibid., pp. 49, 53.

Notes to Chapter 3

1. "Geistige Neigungen in Deutschland" (92a), XI:244.
2. Thomas Mann, *Betrachtungen eines Unpolitischen*, p. 293. Several statements in *Ein Zeitalter wird besichtigt* ([85c], pp. 304-305) show how much importance Heinrich Mann attached to the public representation of literature.
3. *Zwischen den Rassen* (92a), II:144-145; and "Essay über Flaubert" (92a), XI:107.
4. Sartre *(Was ist Literatur?)* and Escarpit *(Das Buch und der Leser)* discussed, the latter under the heading of "creative betrayal," the idea of "mission" as established by Ramón Fernández in his book *Messages*, which appeared in 1926. The best known legend of the twenties was probably the one constructed around the work of Franz Kafka.
5. "Goethe-Feier" (92a), XI:463.
6. Thomas Mann, "Die Unbekannten," *Die Forderung des Tages* (Berlin 1930), pp. 403ff.
7. In regard to the relationship between sociology and philology, compare the positions of H. D. Duncan, *Language and Literature in Society* (Chicago, 1953), pp. viii-ix and 237, n. 5, and H. Kuhn, *Dichtung und Welt im Mittelalter* (Stuttgart, 1959), p. 38.
8. Special concern is given here to parts of the essays "Geistige Neigungen in Deutschland," "Die neuen Gebote," "Unser Enfluss und diese Zeit," "Theater der Zeit," "Die geistige Lage," and "Die Zukunft der Kultur." All of these were composed between 1925 and 1931 (92a), XI:244-245, 249-250, 264-265, 270-271, 349-350; and (92a), XII:378-379.
9. *Ein Zeitalter wird besichtigt* (85c), p. 182.
10. Weisstein, *Heinrich Mann*, pp. 220-221. This novella tells of a couple of young lovers at the carnival in Nice who are lured by a ghostly old man to his castle, where he is later consumed by

fire. It is far more likely that the ironic Heinrich Mann was making parody of the conflict between the generations by using the Hansel-and-Gretel motif. Save for Hermann Kesten, Mann found no new adherents among the young writers of the twenties. Heinrich Mann did, however, find a strong supporter among the young postwar generation in France in the person of Philippe Soupault. This support should not be seen merely as the result of Mann's admiration for French literary traditions in general but also as an offshoot of his "artistic" propensities, as illustrated in chapter 1. Soupault was one of the chief representatives of French surrealism. Although many famous surrealist painters are to be found in Germany, the surrealist school never gained much influence in German literature. As Sartre *(Was ist Literatur?)* has pointed out, surrealism was the final and crowning act of the Nietzschean "reevaluation of values," i.e., the overturning of the traditional life/work relationship described in chapter 1. Thus, Soupault, as a surrealist, could view an "artistic" writer like Mann as a spiritual mentor, much as he might view French "artistic" writers like Flaubert, Baudelaire, the Goncourts, or Maupassant.

11. Heinrich Mann, "Grosse Sache" und "Geist und Tat," *Deutsche Rundschau* (Berlin, 1932), 231:132ff.

12. "Unser Einfluss und diese Zeit" (92a), XI:265, 267-268.

13. "It doesn't matter at all if a writer has public spirit; but it is all-important for him and society whether or not people will read him at later times. Then this single individual, stronger than all social forms of his day, has brought together people who would otherwise have never known one another." ("Essay über Stendhal" [92a] , XI:49.) "In less than thirty years even the prevalent types among people have altered, and nobody will know what life was like in our days. It will be, then, exactly the way the strongest among us has depicted it." ("Die geistige Lage" [92a] , XI:350.)

14. "Beiträge" (50), V/II:458; "Was ist eigentlich ein Schriftsteller? " (92a), XI:309; *Ein Zeitalter wird besichtigt* (85c), p. 187. In an age of various "futurologist" endeavors, English-speaking readers will be sure to notice that "anticipation" is a literal translation of the word "Vorwegnahme," generally used by Mann. Unlike Marx or Saint-Simon with their more or less utopian writings, Mann did not concern himself with what was certain to come about under given conditions (predictions), or

with what is at least probable under given circumstances (forecasts), but, for the most part, with what he assumed to be possible achievements on any chosen terms (anticipations). Once again, the emphasis behind his assumption seems to be due to his conviction not that he should have been more accurate than others in his anticipations but rather that his writings were of a more exemplary kind and value. This flattering verdict undoubtedly resulted both from the feedback of the "Kaiserreich" legend described in chapter 2 on its author and from the "artistic" equation of life and work described in chapter 1.

15. Concerning the prophetic role of Goethe, Balzac, Stendhal, Hugo, Zola, Hauptmann, Wedekind, and Gorki, see (92a), XI: 47, 64, 166-167, 238, 263, 391-392, 396ff., 431.
16. "Die geistige Lage" (92a), XI:350.
17. "Unser Einfluss und diese Zeit" (92a), XI:264.
18. "Theater der Zeit" (92a), XI:274.
19. *Eugénie* (92a), V:19, 29.
20. Ibid., pp. 20, 22, 29-30, 102, 116, 167.
21. Thomas Mann, *Betrachtungen eines Unpolitischen*, p. 161.
22. C. Knoertzer, "Heinrich Manns *Eugénie,*" *Revue Rhénane* (Mainz, 1929), p. 69.
23. *Eugénie* (92a), V:206.
24. "Der bürgerliche Held" (92a), XI:131.
25. "Die Zukunft der Kultur" (92a), XII:380.
26. "Essay über Stendhal" (92a), XI:46.
27. *Es kommt der Tag* (82), p. 200.
28. Ibid., p. 56.
29. Ibid., pp. 62-63, 208, 231.
30. Ibid., pp. 194, 216, 218, 228, 231.
31. Ibid., p. 229.
32. Thomas Mann, *Werke,* Berliner Ausgabe, XI:769. Weisstein (*Heinrich Mann,* p. 191) believes *Der Atem* to be the earlier work, but the listing of works given by Victor Mann (*Wir waren fünf,* p. 613) agrees with our chronology. To be sure, Weisstein (p. 199, n. 26) presents considerable evidence for his view. But this evidence could just as easily be used to support the opposite opinion.
33. *Empfang bei der Welt* (19a), pp. 6, 8, 25, 31, 69, 83, 92, 103, 141.
34. According to the Hauswedell Catalogue (Hamburg, 1960), Pos. 202; the letter to Kantorowicz cited by Jhering (*Heinrich Mann,* p. 146); and *Ein Zeitalter wird besichtigt* (85c), pp. 79, 326.

35. *Der Atem* (18a), pp. 19-22, 48-49, 71, 285. The words "cagoule" and "synarchie," and the name "Lehideux," which appear here, have to do with events that actually occurred around Minister Darlan and the French secret service during World War II.
36. Ibid., p. 200; also *Empfang bei der Welt* (19a), p. 164.
37. *Empfang bei der Welt* (19a), pp. 43, 52, 200, 221-222, 331.
38. Ibid., p. 24.
39. Ibid., p. 356.
40. Ibid., p. 145.
41. *Ein Zeitalter wird besichtigt* (85c), p. 164.
42. *Der Atem* (18a), pp. 151ff.
43. Ibid., p. 159.
44. *Empfang bei der Welt* (19a), pp. 183-184.
45. Ibid., pp. 127ff.
46. Ibid., p. 256.
47. *Der Atem* (18a), p. 352.

Selected Bibliography

Books

Martens, K. *Literatur in Deutschland. Studien und Eindrücke.* Berlin, 1910.
Leonard, R. "Das Werk Heinrich Manns." *Der neue Roman. Ein Almanach.* Leipzig & Munich, 1917.
Edschmid, K. *Die doppelköpfige Nymphe.* Berlin, 1920.
Sinsheimer, H. *Heinrich Manns Werk. Zu seinem 50. Geburtstag.* Munich, 1921.
Soergel, A. "Heinrich Mann." *Dichtung und Dichter der Zeit. Neue Folge: Im Banne des Expressionismus.* Leipzig, 1925.
Bab, J. *Befreiungs-Schlacht. Kulturpolitische Betrachtungen aus literarischen Anlässen.* Stuttgart, 1928.
Bertaux, F. *Panorama de la littérature allemande contemporaine.* Paris, 1928.
Untermann, M. "Das Groteske bei Th. Mann, H. Mann, Morgenstern und W. Busch." Dissertation. Königsberg, 1929.
Liebermann, M.; Grimme, A.; Mann, T. and H.; Benn, G.; Feuchtwanger, L. *Fünf Reden und eine Entgegnung zum 60. Geburtstag.* Berlin, 1931.
Schröder, W. *Heinrich Mann—Bildnis eines Meisters. Eine Monographie.* Vienna, 1931.
Jacobson, A. *Nachklänge Richard Wagners im Roman.* Heidelberg, 1932.
Hiller, K. *Profile. Prosa aus einem Jahrzehnt.* Paris, 1938.
Boonstra, P. E. "Heinrich Mann als politischer Schriftsteller." Dissertation. Utrecht, 1945.

Lemke, K. *Heinrich Mann, Zu Seinem 75. Geburtstag.* Berlin, 1946.

Mann, V. *Wir warren fünf. Bildnis der Familie Mann.* Konstanz, 1949.

Hiller, K. "Heinrich Mann als Publizist." *Köpfe und Tröpfe.* Hamburg, 1950.

Magon, L. "Heinrich Mann" Commenorative speech at the University of Greifswald. Greifswald, 1950.

Mayer, H. *Thomas Mann—Werk und Entwicklung.* Berlin, 1950.

Jhering, H. *Heinrich Mann.* Berlin, 1951.

Kantorowicz, A. *Der Einfluss der Oktober-Revolution auf Heinrich Mann.* Berlin, 1952.

Lutz, G. "Zur Problematik des Spielerischen. Eine Erörterung unter besonderer Berücksichtigung der Romane und Novellen des frühen Heinrich Mann." Dissertation. Freiburg, 1952.

Salzmann, K. H. "Der Verlag Kurt Wolff." *Imprimatur* XI. Hamburg, 1952-1953.

Kantorowicz, A. *Das Vermächtnis Heinrich Manns.* Berlin, 1953.

O'Bear, E. D. "The Significance of France in the Writings of Heinrich Mann." Dissertation. State University, Columbus, Ohio, 1953.

Sears, R. S. "Syntactical Studies in Heinrich Mann." Dissertation. University of Illinois, Glencoe, Ill., 1954.

Specht, G. "Das Problem der Macht bei Heinrich Mann." Dissertation. Freiburg, 1954.

Lukács, G. "Der Kampf zwischen Liberalismus und Demokratie im Spiegel des historischen Romans der deutschen Antifaschisten." *Probleme des Realismus.* Berlin, 1955.

Lukács, G. "Heinrich Manns *Henri Quatre,"* Der historische Roman. Berlin, 1955.

Kantorowicz, A. *Heinrich und Thomas Mann. Die persönlichen, literarischen und weltanschaulichen Beziehungen der Brüder nebst Auswahl ihres Briefwechsels 1900-1927.* Berlin, 1956.

Kirchner-Klemperer, H. "Heinrich Manns Roman 'Jugend und Vollendung des Königs Henri Quatre' im Verhältnis zu seinen Quellen und Vorlagen. Ein Beitrag zum Thema 'Historischer Roman.' " Dissertation. Berlin, 1957.

Mayer, H. "Heinrich Manns *Henri Quatre." Deutsche Literatur und Weltliteratur. Gesammelte Reden und Aufsätze.* Berlin, 1957.

Wsesojusnaja Gosudarstwennaja Biblioteka. *Inostrannoi Literatury. Pisateli Sarubeznych Stran. No. 8 Genrich Mann. Bio-Bibliograficeskii Ukasatelj.* Moscow, 1957.

Manina, G. E. "Publicistika Genricha Manna 40-godov." *Literatura Germanskoj Demokrat. Respubl.* Moscow, 1958.

Herzog, W. *Menschen, denen ich begegnete.* Bern & Munich, 1959.

Kantorowicz, A. *Deutsches Tagebuch.* Munich, 1959.
Kesten, H. *Meine Freunde, die Poeten.* Munich, 1959.
Mazzucchetti, L. "I Sessant' Anni di Heinrich Mann." *Novencento in Germania.* Milan, 1959.
Schöpker, H. F. "Heinrich Mann als Darsteller des Hysterischen und Grotesken." Dissertation. Bonn, 1959.
Sussbach, H. H. "Kritik am Jugendwerk Heinrich Manns." Dissertation. University of Southern California, Los Angeles, Cal., 1959.
Nartov, K. M. *Genrich Mann. Ocerk Tworcestwa.* Moscow, 1960.
Edschmid, K. *Lebendiger Expressionismus.* Vienna, 1961.
Weisstein, U. *Heinrich Mann. Eine historisch-kritische Einführung in sein dichterisches Werk.* Tübingen, 1962.
Eggert, R. *Vorläufiges Findbuch der Werkmanuskripte von Heinrich Mann.* Deutsche Akademie der Künste. Berlin, 1963.
Serebrov, N. N. *Genrich Mann. Ocerk tworceskogo puti.* Moscow, 1964.
Banuls, A. *Heinrich Mann. Le pòete et la politique.* Paris, 1966.
Linn, R. N. *Heinrich Mann.* New York, 1967.
Schröter, K. *Heinrich Mann in Selbstzeugnissen und Bilddokumenten.* Reinbek bei Hamburg, 1967.
Zenker, E. *Heinrich-Mann-Bibliographie. Band 1 Werke.* Berlin und Weimar, 1967.
Wysling, H. *Thomas Mann und Heinrich Mann: Briefwechsel 1900-1949.* Frankfurt/M., 1968.

Magazine Articles

Morgenstern, G. "Heinrich Manns *Familie.*" *Gesellschaft,* no. 12. Munich, 1894.
Oppeln-Bronikowski, F. v. "Heinrich Manns *Ein Verbrechen.*" *Litterarisches Echo,* no. 24. Berlin, 1899.
Ettlinger, J. "Heinrich Manns *Im Schlaraffenland.*" *Litterarisches Echo,* no. 5. Berlin, 1901.
Hart, H. "Heinrich Manns *Im Schlaraffenland.*" *Velhagen & Klasing Monatshefte* I. Leipzig, 1901.
Kalkschmidt, E. "Heinrich Manns *Im Schlaraffenland.*" *Kunstwart* II. Munich, 1901.
Kalkschmidt, E. "Heinrich Manns *Im Schlaraffenland.*" *Lotse,* no. 17. Hamburg, 1902.
Busse, C. "Heinrich Manns *Göttinnen.*" *Deutsche Monatsschrift für das gesamte Leben der Gegenwart,* no. 6. Berlin, 1903.
Danegger, A. "Manns *Jagd nach Liebe.*" *Freistatt,* no. 50. Munich, 1903.

Esswein, H. "Heinrich Manns *Göttinnen.*" *Freistatt,* no. 17. Munich, 1903.

Fred, W. "Heinrich Manns *Göttinnen.*" *Zukunft* 43. Berlin, 1903.

Hart, H. "Heinrich Manns *Göttinnen.*" *Velhagen & Klasings Monatshefte* II. Leipzig, 1903.

Jacobs, M. "Heinrich Manns *Göttinnen.*" *Nation,* no. 32. Berlin, 1903.

Wengraf, R. "Heinrich Manns *Göttinnen.*" *Litterarisches Echo.* no. 24. Berlin, 1903.

Aram, K. "Heinrich Manns *Jagd nach Liebe.*" *Kunstwart* I. Munich, 1904.

Greiner, L. "Heinrich Manns *Jagd nach Liebe.*" *Litterarisches Echo,* no. 16. Berlin, 1904.

Friedrich, P. "Heinrich Mann–Phantasien über einen Phantasten." *Gegenwart* 68. Berlin, 1905.

Speyer, J. "Heinrich Manns *Jagd nach Liebe.*" *Zukunft* 52. Berlin, 1905.

Wendel H. "Heinrich Mann." *Sozialistische Monatshefte* II. Berlin, 1905.

Schaukal, R. v. "Heinrich Manns *Flöten und Dolche* und *Professor Unrat.*" *Litterarisches Echo,* no. 5. Berlin, 1906.

Schickele, R. "Heinrich Manns *Stürmische Morgen.*" *Zukunft* 57. Berlin, 1906.

Böckel, R. "Heinrich Manns *Stürmische Morgen.*" *Literarisches Echo,* no. 13. Berlin, 1907.

Bonsels, W. "Heinrich Manns *Zwischen den Rassen.*" *Zukunft* 60. Berlin, 1907.

Busse, C. "Heinrich Manns *Stürmische Morgen.*" *Velhagen & Klasings Monatshefte* I. Bielefeld, 1907.

Brod, M. "Heinrich Manns *Mnais und Ginevra.*" *Gegenwart* 71. Berlin, 1907.

Brod, M. "Heinrich Manns *Zwischen den Rassen.*" *Gegenwart* 72. Berlin, 1907.

Mühsam, E. "Heinrich Mann." *Blaubuch,* no. 23. Berlin, 1907.

Dülberg, F. "Heinrich Manns *Mnais und Ginevra.*" *Litterarisches Echo,* no. 5. Berlin, 1908.

Frapan-Akunian, I. "Heinrich Manns *Zwischen den Rassen.*" *Litterariches Echo,* no. 14. Berlin, 1908.

Müller-Freienfels, R. "Heinrich Mann." *Österreichische Rundschau* 18. Vienna, 1908.

Sauer, H. "Heinrich Mann." *Litterarisches Echo,* no. 1. Berlin, 1909.

Brand, M. "Heinrich Manns *Kleine Stadt.*" *Schaubühne,* p. 310. Berlin, 1910.

Frost, L. D. "Heinrich Manns *Kleine Stadt.*" *Zukunft* 70. Berlin, 1910.

Mann, H. "Antwort an L. D. Frost." *Zukunft* 70. Berlin, 1910.

Hatvany, L. "Heinrich Manns *Kleine Stadt.*" *Neue Rundschau* III. Berlin, 1910.

Huldschiner, R. "Heinrich Manns *Kleine Stadt.*" *Litterarisches Echo,* no. 14. Berlin, 1910.

Kahn, H. "Heinrich Mann." *Schaubühne,* no. 49. Berlin, 1910.

Rath, W. "Heinrich Manns *Kleine Stadt.*" *Kunstwart* II. Munich, 1910.

Hülsen, H. v. "Heinrich Manns *Das Herz.*" *Litterarisches Echo,* no. 17. Berlin, 1911.

Mühsam, E. "Heinrich Mann." *Aktion,* p. 592. Berlin, 1911.

Kurtz, R. "Heinrich Manns politische Ideologie." *Aktion,* no. 51. Berlin, 1912.

Pick, O. "Die Schauspielerin in der Literatur. Zur Psychologie der Schauspielerin bei H. Mann und E. de Goncourt." *Aktion,* p. 783. Berlin, 1912.

Strecker, K. "Heinrich Manns *Rückkehr vom Hades.*" *Litterarisches Echo,* no. 10. Berlin, 1912.

Benn, G. "Heinrich Mann—Ein Untergang." *Aktion,* no. 16. Berlin, 1913.

Huebner, F. M. "Heinrich Mann—Prognose." *Aktion,* p. 823. Berlin, 1913.

Mann, T. "Der Literat." *März,* no. 1. Munich, 1913.

Mann, T. "Der Künstler und der Literat." *März,* no. 2. Munich, 1913.

Müller-Freienfels, R. "Heinrich Mann und die Gegenwart." *Tat,* no. 12. Jena, 1913.

Huebner, F. M. "Das erotische Problem bei Heinrich Mann." *Schaubühne,* no. 16. Berlin, 1914.

Huebner, F. M. "Heinrich Manns *Untertan.*" *Aktion,* p. 334. Berlin, 1914.

Rubiner, L. "Heinrich Manns *Untertan.*" *Aktion,* p. 335. Berlin, 1914.

Huebner, F. M. "Heinrich Mann wider Dostojewskij." *Schaubühne,* p. 392. Berlin, 1915.

Huebner, F. M. "Der Dichter Heinrich Mann." *Ähre,* no. 38. Zurich, 1915.

Heuss, T. "Die Politisierung des Literaten." *Litterarisches Echo,* no. 11. Berlin, 1916.

Elster, H. M. "Zwischen zwei Meeren. Bemerkungen zum Schaffen Heinrich Manns." *Ähre,* no. 3-4. Zurich, 1916.

Sommerfeld, M. "Der Schulmeister." *Litterarisches Echo,* no. 9. Berlin, 1916.

Beyer, G. "Heinrich Manns *Die Armen.*" *Glocke* II. Berlin, 1917.

Fontana, O. M. "Heinrich Manns *Die Armen.*" *Wage,* no. 40. Vienna, 1917.

Friedenthal, J. "H. Mann." *März,* no. 22. Munich, 1917.

Goll, I. "Les deux Mann." *Semaine littéraire,* no. 1233. Geneva, 1917.

Mhe, H. "Heinrich Manns *Die Armen.*" *Literarische Gesellschaft,* no. 11-12. Hamburg, 1917.

Moreck, C. "H. Mann." *Glocke* I. Berlin, 1917.

Bry, K. C. "Heinrich Manns *Die Armen.*" *Das neue Deutschland,* no. 7. Gotha, 1918.

Diederich, F. "Heinrich Manns *Die Armen.*" *Die neue Zeit* I. Berlin, 1918.

Froberger, J. "Heinrich Mann." *Bücherwelt,* no. 12. Cologne, 1918.

Heine, A. "Heinrich Manns Führerberuf. Eine Betrachtung anlässlich seines Romans *Die Armen.*" *Litterarisches Echo,* p. 377. Berlin, 1918.

Kahn, H. "Heinrich Manns *Die Armen.*" *Weltbühne* I. Berlin, 1918.

Rubiner, L. "Heinrich Manns *Die Armen.*" *Aktion,* no. 3-4. Berlin, 1918.

Steiger, E. "Heinrich Manns *Die Armen.*" *Die neue Zeit* I. Berlin, 1918.

Strecker, K. "Heinrich Manns *Die Armen.*" *Velhagen & Klasings Monatshefte* I. Bielefeld, 1918.

Bartels, A. "Heinrich Manns *Untertan.*" *Konservative Monatsschrift,* no. 6. Berlin, 1919.

Diederich, F. "Heinrich Manns *Untertan.*" *Die neue Zeit* II. Berlin, 1919.

Eloesser, A. "Heinrich Manns *Untertan.*" *Deutsche Rundschau* 180. Berlin, 1919.

Helmolt, H. F. "Das wilhelminische Kaisertum und sein Untertan." *Europäische Staats– und Wirtschaftszeitung,* p. 594. Berlin, 1919.

Mahrholz, W. "Heinrich Manns *Untertan.*" *Litterarisches Echo,* no. 9. Berlin, 1919.

Thorn, E. "Heinrich Mann." *Literarische Gesellschaft,* no. 7-8. Hamburg, 1919.

Tucholsky (I. Wrobel), K. "Heinrich Manns *Untertan.*" *Weltbühne* I. Berlin, 1919.

Boek, F. "H. Manns politisches Glaubensbekenntnis." *Preussische Jahrbücher* 182. Berlin, 1920.

Elster, H. M. "Heinrich Manns politisches Bekenntnis." *Das neue Buch,* no. 2. Berlin, 1920.

Graetzer, F. "Heinrich Manns *Die Ehrgeizige.*" *Litterarisches Echo,* no. 23. Berlin, 1920.

Endres, F. C. "Das Werk Heinrich Manns." *Wissen und Leben,* p. 641. Zurich, 1921.

Friedenthal, J.; Ewers, L.; et al. "Geburtstagsadressen zum 50. Geburtstag Heinrich Manns." *Litterarisches Echo,* no. 15. Berlin, 1921.

Sinsheimer, H. "Das Problem Heinrich Mann." *Initiale,* no. 3. Vienna, 1921.

Bertaux, F. "L'influence de Zola en Allemagne." *Revue de littérature comparée,* no. 1. Paris, 1924.

Haas, W. "Heinrich Manns Europa—Reich über den Reichen." *Neue Rundschau* I. Berlin, 1924.

Muckermann, F. "Dichtung und Grossindustrie." *Gral,* no. 6. Essen, 1924.

Dürr, E. "Zur Neuausgabe von Heinrich Manns *In einer Familie.*" *Literatur,* no. 8. Berlin, 1925.

Flake, O. "Heinrich Manns *Der Kopf.*" *Neue Rundschau* II. Berlin, 1925.

Mann, T. "Heinrich Mann's *Der Kopf.*" *The Dial,* p. 335. New York, 1925.

Posselt, E. "Heinrich Mann's *Der Kopf.*" *Saturday Review of Literature,* p. 87. New York, 1925.

Spenlé, J.-E. "Heinrich Manns *Kaiserreich-Trilogie.*" *Mercure de France* 184. Paris, 1925.

Bertaux, F. "Heinrich Mann et les lettres françaises." *Europe* 10. Paris, 1925-1926.

Bertaux, F. "Heinrich Manns *Der Kopf.*" *Nouvelle Revue Française,* no. 145. Paris, 1926.

Bertaux, F. "Heinrich Manns *Liliane und Paul.*" *Nouvelle Revue Française,* no. 154. Paris, 1926.

Brock, E. "Die Brüder Mann auf der Wallfahrt nach Europa." *Gewissen,* no. 14. Berlin, 1926.

Dürr, E. "Der Selbstmord des Kopfes." *Literatur,* no. 2. Berlin, 1926.

Heilborn, E. "Heinrich Manns *Liliane und Paul.*" *Literatur,* no. 9. Berlin, 1926.

Diebold, B. "Heinrich Manns *Mutter Marie.*" *Literatur,* no. 8. Berlin, 1927.

Fontana, O. M. "Heinrich Manns *Mutter Marie.*" *Tagebuch,* no. 14. Berlin, 1927.

Mehring, W. "Kleine Nachtischrede an Heinrich Mann." *Tagebuch,* no. 53. Berlin, 1927.

Demosthenes. "Heinrich Mann und die kommunistische Propaganda." *Deutscher Spiegel,* no. 44. Berlin, 1928.

Offenburg, K. "Heinrich Mann." *Deutsche Republik* I. Frankfurt & Berlin, 1928.

Pohl, G. "Heinrich Mann—Deutschlands erster Epiker. Bemerkungen zu seinem Lebenswerk." *Neue Bücherschau,* no. 1. Berlin, 1928.

Rutra, A. E. "Heinrich Mann in Paris." *Literarische Welt,* no. 3. Berlin, 1928.

Herzog, W. "Heinrich Manns *Sieben Jahre.*" *Literarische Welt,* no. 32. Berlin, 1929.

Kesten, H. "Heinrich Mann." *Weltbühne* II. Berlin, 1929.

Knoertzer, C. "Heinrich Manns *Eugénie.*" *Revue Rhénane,* no. 10. Mainz, 1929.

Lee, R. "Heinrich Manns *Schlaraffenland* in englischer Übersetzung." *Bookman,* p. 195. Manchester, Mass., 1929.

Martens, K. "Heinrich Manns *Eugénie.*" *Die schöne Literatur,* p. 64. Leipzig, 1929.

Rehm, W. "Der Renaissancekult um 1900 und seine Überwindung." *Zeitschrift für deutsche Philologie,* p. 296. Berlin, 1929.

Daniel-Rops, H. "Heinrich Manns *Untertan* in französischer Übersetzung." *Les Nouvelles Littéraires.* Paris, June 8, 1929.

Weltmann, L. "Heinrich Manns *Eugénie.*" *Literatur,* no. 7. Berlin, 1929.

Weltmann, L. "Heinrich Manns *Sieben Jahre.*" *Literatur,* no. 10. Berlin, 1929.

Celsus. "Heinrich Manns *Prof. Unrat* als Film." *Weltbühne* I. Berlin, 1930.

Diamond, W. "Heinrich Mann." *Monatshefte für deutschen Unterricht,* p. 134. Milwaukee, Wisconsin, 1930.

Kesten, H. "Heinrich Manns *Grosse Sache.*" *Weltbühne* II. Berlin, 1930.

Mann, T. "Heinrich Manns *Grosse Sache.*" *Literarische Welt,* no. 50. Berlin, 1930.

Meissinger, K. A. "Heinrich Manns *Sieben Jahre.*" *Deutsche Republik* I. Frankfurt & Berlin, 1930.

Süskind, W. E. "Heinrich Manns *Sie sind jung.*" *Literatur,* no. 7. Berlin, 1930.

Weltmann, L. "Heinrich Manns *Prof. Unrat* als Film." *Literatur,* no. 9. Berlin, 1930.

Benn, G.; Schickele, R.; et al. "Geburtstagsadressen zum 60. Geburtstag Heinrich Manns." *Literatur,* no. 8. Berlin, 1931.

Benn, G. "Heinrich Mann." *Literarische Welt,* no. 13. Berlin, 1931.

Hegemann, W. "Heinrich Mann? Hitler? Gottfried Benn? Oder Goethe? " *Tagebuch,* no. 15. Berlin, 1931.

Kenter, H. D. "Heinrich Manns *Grosse Sache.*" *Literatur,* no. 4. Berlin, 1931.

Kuttner, E. "Heinrich Mann." *Der Staat seid Ihr,* no. 4. Berlin, 1931.

Leonhard, R. "Das Werk Heinrich Manns." *Neue Rundschau* I. Berlin, 1931.

Weltmann, L. "Heinrich Manns *Geist und Tat.*" *Literatur,* no. 11. Berlin, 1931.

Zeitler, A. "Heinrich Manns *Untertan* auf dem Auslandsmarkt." *Das deutsche Buch,* p. 97. Leipzig, 1931.

Becher, J. R. "Vom *Untertan* zum Untertan." *Linkskurve,* no. 4. Berlin, 1932.

Bergengruen, W. "Heinrich Manns *Grosse Sache* und *Geist und Tat.*" *Deutsche Rundschau* 231. Berlin, 1932.

Hegemann, W. "W. Bloem contra H. Mann." *Tagebuch,* no. 41. Berlin, 1932.

Hiller, K. "Der Präsident." *Weltbühne* I. Berlin, 1932.

Jellinek, F. "Heinrich Manns *Öffentliches Leben.*" *Tagebuch,* no. 33. Berlin, 1932.

Kesten, H. "Heinrich Manns *Ernstes Leben.*" *Literarische Welt,* no. 45. Berlin, 1932.

Weltmann, L. "Heinrich Manns *Öffentliches Leben.*" *Literatur,* no. 10. Berlin, 1932.

Wutkowski, H. "H. und T. Mann als deutsche Politiker." *Deutschen Spiegel,* no. 11. Berlin, 1932.

Milch, W. "Heinrich Manns *Ernstes Leben.*" *Literatur,* no. 5. Berlin, 1933.

Feuchtwanger, L. "Heinrich Manns *Jugend des Königs Henri Quatre.*" *Das neue Tagebuch,* p. 65. Paris & Amsterdam, 1936.

Rosenhaupt, H. W. "Heinrich Mann und die Gesellschaft." *Germanic Review,* p. 267. New York, 1937.

Bianquis, G. "Problèmes sociaux dans le roman allemand contemporain." *Revue de cours et conférences,* p. 21. Paris, 1938.

Ewnin, A. "Der Geschichtsroman Heinrich Manns." *Oktjabr,* no. 3. Moscow, 1938.

Lukács, G. "Heinrich Manns *Henri Quatre.*" *Das Wort,* no. 8. Moscow, 1938.

Gross, F. "Heinrich Mann." *Contemporary Review,* p. 120. London, 1941.

Kayser, R. "Heinrich Mann." *Books Abroad,* p. 401. Norman, Okla., 1941.

Hofe, H. v. "German Literature in Exile: Heinrich Mann." *German Quarterly,* p. 88. Lancaster, Pa., 1944.

Kiewert, W. "Heinrich Manns *Lidice.*" *Weltbühne,* p. 392. Berlin, 1947.

Kiewert, W. "Heinrich Mann und die französische Kultur." *Berliner Hefte für geistiges Leben,* p. 197. Berlin, 1947.

Laureillard, G. "Heinrich Mann." *Lancelot,* no. 5. Neuwied, 1947.

Luft, F. "Heinrich Manns *Ein Zeitalter wird besichtigt.*" *Ost und West,* no. 5. Berlin, 1947.

Reinke, C. "Heinrich Manns *Untertan*–Spiegel des Kommenden." *Denkendes Volk*, p. 138. Berlin, Braunschweig & Hamburg, 1947.

Schröder, W. "Heinrich Mann der Deutsche." *Ost und West*, p. 9. Berlin, 1947.

Weiskopf, F. C. "Heinrich Mann, Der grosse Lehrer." *Weltbühne*, p. 236. Berlin, 1947.

Blachstein, P. "H. Mann besichtigt sein Zeitalter." *Hamburger akademische Rundschau*, no. 7-8. Hamburg, 1948.

Bihali-Merin, O. "Hajnrich Mann. Beleske povodom negove smrti." *Knizevnost*, p. 478. Belgrade, 1950.

Feuchtwanger, L. et al. "Nachruf auf Heinrich Mann." *Kulturaufbau*, p. 136. Düsseldorf, 1950.

Georgieva, N. "Hajnrich Mann." *Semptemvri*, p. 137. Sofia, 1950.

Grosshut, F. S. "Heinrich Mann." *Books Abroad*, no. 4. Norman, Okla., 1950.

Mann, T. "Bericht über meinen Bruder." *Germanic Review*, p. 243. New York, 1950.

Mann, T. "Bericht über meinen Bruder." *Aufbau*, p. 305. Berlin, 1950.

Rost, N. "Heinrich Mann als politischer Schriftsteller." *Forum*, no. 1. Amsterdam, 1950.

Rilke, R. M. "Heinrich Manns *Zwischen den Rassen.*" Letter to Mme. L. Albert-Lasard, 1916. *Les Nouvelles Littéraires.* Paris, April 27, 1950.

Sieburg, F. "Flöten und Dolche. Zum Tode von H. Mann." *Gegenwart*, no. 7. Freiburg, Br., 1950.

Zweig, A. "Nachruf auf Heinrich Mann." *Aufbau*, p. 295. Berlin, 1950.

Berger, U. "Heinrich Manns *Die Armen.*" *Aufbau*, p. 664. Berlin, 1951.

Brandl, B. "Heinrich Mann 1871-1950." *Bibliothekar*, p. 350. Leipzig & Berlin, 1951.

Kantorowicz, A. "Heinrich Manns *Henri Quatre.*" *Sinn und Form*, no. 5. Potsdam, 1951.

Kantorowicz, A. "Das frühe Werk Heinrich Manns." *Aufbau*, p. 1087. Berlin, 1951.

Lemke, K. "Heinrich-Mann-Renaissance?" *Deutsche Woche*, no. 5. Munich, 1951.

Sielaff, E. "Heinrich Mann–Kritiker, Realist, Humanist." *Heute und Morgen*, pp. 170, 739, Schwerin, 1951.

Buckow, B. S. "Genrich Mann. Pamjati pistalja-demokrata." *Ogonek*, no. 12. Moscow, 1952.

Drews, R. "Heinrich Manns Vermächtnis." *Weltbühne*, p. 120. Berlin, 1952.

Linn, R. N. "The place of 'Pippo Spano' in the work of Heinrich Mann." *Modern Language Forum*, p. 130. Los Angeles, 1952.

Rilke, R. M. "Heinrich Manns *Zwischen den Rassen.*" Albert-Lasard, L. *Wege mit Rilke.* Frankfurt, 1952.

Siedler, W. J. "Heinrich Mann oder der Glaube an die Macht der Vernunft." *Neue literarische Welt,* no. 1. Heidelberg, 1952.

Werner, V. "Dva pohledy na dílo Heinricha Manna." *Casopis pro moderní filologii,* p. 246. Prague, 1953.

Hardaway, R. T. "Heinrich Mann's *Kaiserreich-Trilogy* and the Democratic Spirit." *Journal of English and German Philology,* no. 12. Urbana, III., 1954.

Kantorowicz, A. "Heinrich Mann—Vorkämpfer deutsch-französischer Verständigung." *Aufbau,* p. 215. Berlin, 1954.

Kantorowicz, A. "Heinrich Manns Essay über Zola als Brennpunkt der weltanschaulichen Beziehungen zwischen H. und T. Mann." *Neue deutsche Literatur,* no. 5. Berlin, 1955.

Linn, R. N. "Portrait of two Despots by H. M." *Germanic Review,* p. 125. New York, 1955.

Mann, T. "Bericht über meinen Bruder." *Werke.* Berlin, 1955.

Montigny, R. "H. Mann und Frankreich." *Antares,* no. 1. Baden-Baden, 1955.

Rost, N. "Bij de dood van T. Mann." *Vrede,* no. 33. Vrede, 1955.

Schräpel, J. "Heinrich Mann—Ein Vergessener." *Dokumentation,* p. 132. Hanover, 1955.

Kirsch, E. "Heinrich Manns historischer Roman *Jugend und Vollendung des Königs Henri Quatre.*" *Wissenschaftliche Zeitschrift der Martin-Luther-Universität.* Gesellschafts— und Sprachwissenschaftliche Reihe, p. 623. Halle-Wittenberg, 1955-1956.

Albrechtova, G. "K vyroci smrti Thomase Manna." *Casopis pro moderní filologii,* p. 63. Prague, 1957.

Kantorowicz, A. "Heinrich Manns Beitrag zur deutsch-französischen Verständigung." *Wissenschaftliche Zeitschrift der Humboldt-Universität.* Gesellschafts— und Sprachwissenschaftliche Reihe, p. 29. Berlin, 1956-1957.

Marcuse, L. "Ich plädiere für Heinrich Mann—An die Verleger, Buchhändler und Leser, die er in Westdeutschland nicht hat." *Zeit,* no. 22. Hamburg, 1957.

Pross, H. "Heinrich Mann—Der letzte Jakobiner," *Deutsche Rundschau,* p. 1050. Baden-Baden, 1957.

Benn, G. "Heinrich Mann—Ein Untergang." *Prosa und Szenen.* D. Wellershoff, ed. Wiesbaden, 1958.

Linn, R. N. "Heinrich Manns *Die Branzilla.*" *Monatshefte für deutschen Unterricht,* p. 75. Madison, Wis., 1958.

Schär, P. "Das doppelte Unrecht an H. Mann." *Weltwoche,* no. 1292. Zurich, 1958.

Schroers, P. "H. und T. Mann und ihre Verleger. Hinweise auf zwei Briefe und eine Briefsammlung." *Philobiblon,* p. 310. Hamburg, 1958.

Uhse, B. "Fragmentarische Bemerkungen zum Friedrich-Fragment Heinrich Manns." *Sinn und Form,* p. 238. Berlin, 1958.

Weissbach, G. "Heinrich Mann: Essays aus dem Nachlass." *Aufbau,* p. 499. Berlin, 1958.

Bachmair, H. F. "Die Leidenschaften der Herzogin von Assy. Zur Entstehungsgeschichte von Heinrich Manns Roman *Die Göttinnen.*" *Philobiblon,* p. 142. Hamburg, 1959.

Kesten, H. "H. und T. Mann." *Monat,* no. 125. Berlin, 1959.

Kesten, H. "Heinrich Manns *Henri Quatre.*" *Weltwoche,* no. 1329. Zurich, 1959.

Weisstein, U. "Heinrich Manns *Henri Quatre.*" *Monatshefte für deutschen Unterricht,* p. 13. Madison, Wis., 1959.

Weisstein, U. "Heinrich Mann in America. A Critical Survey." *Books Abroad,* p. 281. Norman, Okla., 1959.

Exner, R. "Heinrich Manns Essayistik," *Symposium* XIII, 1959, and 1960, p. 26. Syracuse, N.Y.

Frenzel, C. O. "Heinrich Mann—Ein militanter Humanist." *Volksbühne,* p. 162. Hamburg, 1960.

Henschel, P. "H. Mann. Zu seinem 10. Todestag." *Lübeckische Blätter,* p. 65, 1960.

Kamnitzer, H. "Heinrich Manns Essays im Exil." *Neue deutsche Literatur,* p. 91. Berlin, 1960.

Kantorowicz, A. "Zola-Essay und *Betrachtungen eines Unpolitischen.* Die paradigmatische Auseinandersetzung zwischen H. und Th. Mann." *Geschichte in Wissenschaft und Unterricht,* p. 257. Stuttgart, 1960.

Kantorowicz, A. "Das letzte Jahrzehnt Heinrich Manns." *Das Schönste,* no. 3. Munich, 1960.

Kirsch, E., Schmidt, H. "Zur Entstehung von Heinrich Manns *Untertan.*" *Weimarer Beiträge,* p. 112. 1960.

Middelstaedt, W. "H. Mann. Warner, Kritiker und Kämpfer im Spiegel seiner Essays." *Deutschunterricht,* p. 124. Berlin, 1960.

Tucholsky (I. Wrobel), K. "Heinrich Manns *Untertan.*" *Gesammelte Werke.* Gerold-Tucholsky, M. and Raddatz, F. J., eds. Hamburg, 1960.

Nicholls, R. A. "Heinrich Mann and Nietzsche." *Modern Language Quarterly*, p. 165. Seattle, Wash., 1960.

Urbanowicz, M. "Das Bürgertum und der Arbeiter in den Romanen von H. Mann." *Germanica Wratislaviensia*, p. 97. Wroclaw, 1960.

Weisstein, U. "Heinrich Mann's *Kleine Stadt.*" *German Life and Letters*, p. 255. Oxford, 1960.

Weisstein,U. *"Die arme Tonietta*, Heinrich Mann's Triple Version of an Operatic Plot." *Modern Language Quarterly*, p. 371. Seattle, Wash., 1960.

Linn, R. N. "Heinrich Mann and the German Inflation." *Modern Language Quarterly*, p. 75. Seattle, Wash., 1962.

Works Dealing with Literary Sociology

Cassagne, A. *La théorie de l'art pour l'art en France chez les derniers romantiques et les premiers réalistes.* Paris, 1906.

Pareto, V. *Le mythe vertuiste et la littérature immorale.* Paris, 1911.

Baldensperger, F. *La littérature: création, succès, durée.* Paris, 1913.

Schücking, L. L. "Literaturgeschichte und Geschmacksgeschichte." *Germanistisch-Romanistische Monatsschrift*, Berlin, 1913.

Schücking, L. L. "Literaturgeschichte und Geschmacksgeschichte." *Preussische Jbb.* 168. Berlin, 1917.

Einstein, N. *Der Erfolg: Ein Beitrag zur Frage der Vergesellschaftung.* Frankfurt, 1919.

Schücking, L. L. *Die Soziologie der literarischen Geschmacksbildung.* Munich, 1923.

Needham, H. A. *Le développment de l'esthétique sociologique en France et en Angleterre au XIXème siècle.* Paris, 1926.

Hirsch, A. "Soziologie und Literaturgeschichte." *Euphorion.* Stuttgart, 1928.

König, R. *Die naturalistische Ästhetik in Frankreich und ihre Auflösung. Ein Beitrag zur systemwissenschaftlichen Betrachtung der Künstlerästhetik.* Leipzig, 1931.

Schücking, L. L. *Die Soziologie der literarischen Geschmacksbildung.* Leipzig & Berlin, 1931.

Löwenthal, R. "Zur gesellschaftlichen Lage der Literatur." *Zeitschrift für Sozialforschung.* Frankfurt, 1932.

Lützeler, H. "Probleme der Literatursoziologie." *Die neueren Sprachen.* Marburg, 1932.

Lewis, W. "Detachment and the Fictionist." *English Review.* London, 1934.

Hunt, E. L. "The Social Interpretation of Literature." *English Journal.* Chicago, 1935.

Johann, E. *Die deutschen Buchverlage des Naturalismus und der Neuromantik,* Weimar, 1935.

Guérard, A. L. *Art for Art's Sake.* Boston, 1936.

Miller, R. A. "The Relation of Reading Characteristics to Social Indexes." *American Journal of Sociology* VI. Chicago, 1936.

Calmberg, E. "Die Auffassung vom Beruf des Dichters im Weltbild deutscher Dichtung zwischen Nietzsche und George." Dissertation. Tübingen, 1937.

König, R. "Literarische Geschmacksbildung." *Das deutsche Wort.* Berlin, 1937.

Daiches, D. *Language and Society.* London, 1938.

Inglis, R. A. "An Objective Approach to the Relation between Fiction and Society." *American Sociological Review.* Menasha, Wis., 1938.

Park, R. E. "Reflections on Communication and Culture." *American Journal of Sociology.* Chicago, 1938.

Witte, W. "The Sociological Approach to Literature." *Modern Language Review.* Cambridge, 1941.

Doutrepont, G. *La littérature et la societé.* Brussels, 1942.

Muller, H. "Two Major Approaches to the Social Psychology of Reading." *Library Quarterly.* Chicago, 1942.

Levin, H. "Literature as an Institution." *Accent.* Urbana, Ill., 1946.

Schücking, L. L. "Literaturgeschichte und Geschmacksgeschichte." *Essays.* Wiesbaden, 1948.

Caillois, R. *L'homme et le sacré.* Paris, 1950.

Kuhn, H. "Dichtungswissenschaft und Soziologie," *Studium Generale.* Berlin, Göttingen & Heidelberg, 1950.

Caillois, R. *Quatre essais de sociologie contemporaine.* Paris, 1951.

Ziegenfuss, W. *J. J. Rousseau. Eine soziologische Studie.* Erlangen, 1952.

Duncan, H. D. *Language and Literature in Society. A Sociological Essay on Theory and Method in the Interpretation of Linguistic Symbols with a Bibliographical Guide to the Sociology of Literature.* Chicago, 1953.

Hauser, A. *Sozialgeschichte der Kunst und Literatur.* Munich, 1953.

Sartre, J. –P. *Was ist Literatur? Ein Essay.* Hamburg, 1958.

Schöffler, H. *Protestantismus und Literatur.* Göttingen, 1958.

Kayser, W. "Das literarische Leben der Gegenwart." *Deutsche Literatur in unserer Zeit.* Göttingen, 1959.

Kuhn, H. *Dichtung und Welt im Mittelalter.* Stuttgart, 1959.

Escarpit, R. *Das Buch und der Leser. Entwurf einer Literatursoziologie.* Cologne & Opladen, 1961.

Schücking, L. L. *Die Soziologie der literarischen Geschmacksbildung.* Bern & Munich, 1961.

Lukács, G. *Schriften zur Literatursoziologie.* P. Ludz, ed. Neuwied, 1961.

Löwenthal, L. *Literatur und Gesellschaft.* Neuwied, 1964.

Index